BOOK TWO:
REPLICATING ANTIQUE QUILTS

TREASURES
from Yesteryear

SHARON NEWMAN

That Patchwork Place®

Credits

Editor-in-Chief .... Barbara Weiland
Technical Editor .... Janet White
Managing Editor .... Greg Sharp
Copy Editor .... Liz McGehee
Proofreader .... Leslie Phillips
Illustrators .... Carolyn Kraft
                                        Laurel Strand
Illustration Assistant .... Lisa McKenney
Photographer .... Brent Kane
Design Director .... Judy Petry
Text and Cover Designer .... Cheryl Stevenson
Design Assistant .... Claudia L'Heureux
Cover Cat .... Samantha

Treasures from Yesteryear, Book Two:
Replicating Antique Quilts
© 1995 by Sharon L. Newman
That Patchwork Place, Inc., PO Box 118,
Bothell, WA 98041-0118 USA

Printed in Hong Kong
00 99 98 97 96 95   6 5 4 3 2 1

Library of Congress Cataloging-in-Publication Data

(Revised for vol. 2)

Newman, Sharon
    Treasures from yesteryear .

    1. Quilting—Patterns. 2. Patchwork—Patterns. 3. Strip quilting—Patterns.
I. Title
TT835.N476   1995   746.46   94-38618
ISBN 1-56477-039-7 (v. 1 : pbk.)
ISBN 1-56477-063-x (v. 2 : pbk.)

Acknowledgments

My grateful appreciation goes to these quilt caretakers who have preserved the continuing heritage of traditional quiltmaking by sharing this handwork of previous generations: Eleanor Bartholomew, Karen Sikes Collins, Tracy Newman Faulkner, and Diana McClendon. Many thanks to these quiltmakers, who have graciously loaned their replicated quilts to be photographed: Paula A. Baimbridge, Barbara Phiffer, and Doris Gates Taylor.

Special appreciation for reproduction and vintage fabrics is extended to fellow fabric fanatics: Inez Adams, Catherine Anthony, Eugenia Barnes, Sonja Bray, Donna Murray, Barbara Phiffer, Paul Pilgrim, Jackie Reis, Gerald Roy, Eileen Trestain, Peggy Vannoy, and Louise Wood.

Exceptional quilting services were provided by Anne Brann (Animal Friends and Time Passes); Sonja Bray (Sun and Shade); Traci Cowan (Mosaic #17, 1993); Carrie Lou Holtman (Railroad Crossing); Linda Joiner (Reflection of the Past); Sybil Marquis (Barnraising Squares); and Betty Royal (Stars and Bars, Log Cabin in Bars Setting).

The quilts for the book would not have been completed without hours of cutting by Julia Templer, Tracy Faulkner, and Sonja Bray; marking by Etta McFarland; binding by Doris Hagens; scrap patchwork by Sue McGann; and continuous encouragement from Roxi Eppler, Carrie Lou Holtman, Denise Kyle, Carol Newman, and Barbara Phiffer. Jackie Reis of Accu-Pattern Drafting Service has provided special assistance in every area—drafting patterns, making templates, computing yardage, suggesting settings, planning quilting designs, and reminding me to eat! Vicki Newman Potts generously gave editorial assistance and hours of proofreading.

Contents

Dedication

Treasures from Yesteryear, Book Two *is dedicated to my daughters, Tracy Lynne Faulkner, Vicki Lea Potts, and Carol Anne Newman. I cherish the relationship we now have as friends since they have become adults. Their encouragement helped me complete the quilts for this book.*

Introduction

In January of 1979, I opened a specialty shop for quiltmakers. In addition to selling cotton fabrics, quilting books, and hundreds of patterns, my shop offers custom quiltmaking services. We provide design, cutting, patchwork, appliqué, marking, quilting, and binding services. From the beginning, customers also brought quilts for repair or restoration. One of the first quilts brought in for repair was so very worn that restoration was out of the question. The owner of the quilt already knew that was probably the case but wanted a tangible reminder of the family keepsake. When I suggested making a copy of the quilt that would be new and usable, the customer was delighted. I have duplicated other quilts and assisted many quiltmakers in replicating family quilts. This book will share those experiences.

The focus of this second volume of *Treasures from Yesteryear* is the replication of antique quilts. Replication can mean simply reproducing an old block pattern or using antique and/or reproduction fabrics to re-create a quilt that matches the original.

Generations of quiltmakers, sewing patterns from treasured old quilts, preserved many of the stitching techniques and beautiful antique quilt designs still admired today. Replication of the patterns in old quilts has helped preserve the thousands of quilt-block patterns recorded to date. Quiltmakers have always copied patterns; consider the long-term popularity of the Star, Log Cabin, and Double Wedding Ring designs. Before patterns were printed and published, a quilter shared a design by making an actual stitched block, called a "pattern block." (See *Treasures from Yesteryear, Book One*, page 58.) In addition, many quiltmakers have "drawn off" designs from old, worn quilts by sketching or tracing the shapes. Variations in patterns developed as new quiltmakers copied, miscopied, adapted, and altered designs, or simply recolored the same shapes within a pattern.

The hundreds of versions of the favorite "Sunbonnet Sue" demonstrate the tendency of quilters to personalize a pattern. The complexity of the modified design may tell something about the quiltmaker, too. Little girls with two feet, tiny hands, and detailed embroidery contrast with the simple bonnet, dress, and one-shoe version. One may wonder how different the two quiltmakers were as well.

Replicating the pattern and setting of a quilt helps preserve the unique styles of an era, such as whole cloth, appliqué-in-blocks, or medallion quilts. In addition, as the patterns and settings are stitched in new colors and prints, older patterns are revived, and renewed interest emerges. For example, the early twentieth-century quiltmaking revival was based on the so called "colonial" styles from the previous century sewn in new 1920s and 1930s colors and fabrics.

Creating an exact duplication of a quilt is definitely the most demanding form of replication. Matching the pattern and style of a quilt with the appropriate fabric choices produces authenticity in the replica but requires careful research and diligent fabric hunting. (See suggestions for fabric hunting on page 10.) Although the most exact duplication would include reproducing even the quilting design, improvements in batting quality have changed the criteria for selecting a design. Consequently, a contemporary copy of a vintage quilt may require more or less quilting to ensure a stable, durable quilt.

Just as there are various levels of replication, there are also various reasons for reproducing quilts. For example, replicating a family quilt that is worn or too small for the intended use creates a sense of legacy around both the old and the new quilt. In addition, there seems to be an almost timeless and universal appeal in duplicating an admired or well-loved object. Perhaps it is related to the idea that making a copy of a beautiful quilt will result in another beautiful quilt. Duplicating a well-liked pattern can also allow for individual creativity through small variations. Finally, reproducing an unusual or special pattern preserves its uniqueness for another generation.

The Lady of the Lake pattern, named after Sir Walter Scott's 1810 poem, was documented by Ruth E. Finley in *Old Patchwork Quilts and the Women Who Made Them.*

During the early years of the nineteenth century, America imported with enthusiasm English novels and writings of all kinds. Scott's heroic tales particularly pleased men and women of pioneer instincts. And the women of the land honored the author in their most practiced method of artistic self-expression—patchwork.[1]

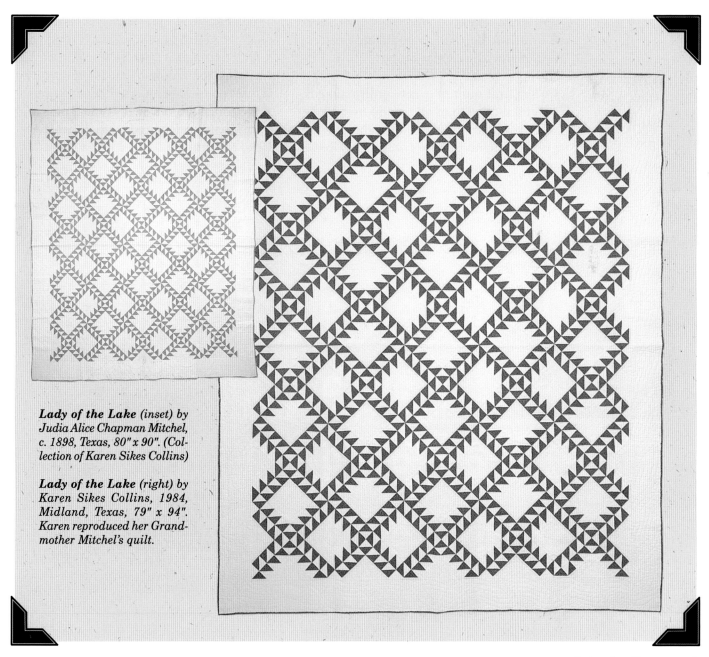

Lady of the Lake (inset) by Judia Alice Chapman Mitchel, c. 1898, Texas, 80" x 90". (Collection of Karen Sikes Collins)

Lady of the Lake (right) by Karen Sikes Collins, 1984, Midland, Texas, 79" x 94". Karen reproduced her Grandmother Mitchel's quilt.

Judia Alice Chapman Mitchel made a Lady of the Lake quilt, probably just before her marriage in 1898. Judia's father, Texas Ranger Ike Chapman, forbade her to marry until she was eighteen years old. Judia's choice of husband-to-be did not please her parents. Cliff Mitchel captured and broke wild horses for a meager livelihood. On her eighteenth birthday, Judia sent word to Cliff to come for her.

Most of her adult life, Judia grew a small plot of long staple cotton, which was ginned separately from the more commonly grown short staple cotton. With longer cotton fibers in her quilt bats, she didn't have to quilt so closely. The red print and white background of this quilt create a dramatic design. The quilting pattern is a grid with original designs quilted in the open areas.

The first quilt of a new quiltmaker is often a duplicate of one made by a close relative or a friend. Granddaughters copy grandmothers' patterns when they have the opportunity to learn how to do the special handwork they have observed. In 1984, Karen Collins reproduced her Grandmother Mitchel's piecing design using a blue cotton print but created her own feather-circle quilting design to fit the open spaces of the pattern.

Karen says, "I enjoy the old 'Lady of the Lake' on a quilt rack; she is too fragile to use for bedcover. But my new Lady sometimes adorns our guest bed." (You can find a pattern for a 12" Lady of the Lake block on page 121 of *Pieces of the Past* by Nancy J. Martin.)

Replacing a very worn quilt with a new and usable one is the reason elderly Mrs. Davis called me in 1980. Her grandson, she reported, had used a family quilt with a Goldfish pattern while working on his car, and "just ruined that old quilt." The fabrics chosen for the replica, including a muslin background, a navy blue solid, and a tiny print of deep red, were characteristic of the late 1890s.

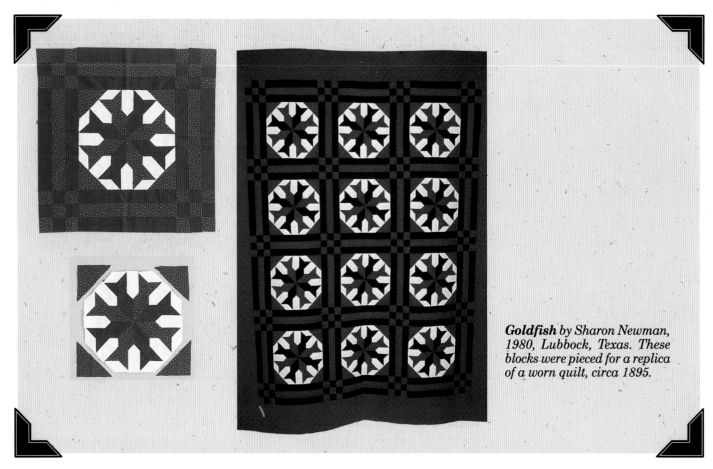

***Goldfish** by Sharon Newman, 1980, Lubbock, Texas. These blocks were pieced for a replica of a worn quilt, circa 1895.*

There were twelve blocks in the original quilt and when I had pieced the fish units, I compared them to the originals before sewing on the corners to complete the blocks. I had Mrs. Davis come back to help me decide whether to position all the navy blue fish the same way or as they were in the original quilt: five blocks with one orientation and seven with another. Mrs. Davis asked me how I would make the quilt, and with my preference for precision, I said I would sew all twelve alike. She interpreted my answer to mean that I would sew the "correct" pattern and that the original was wrong. She began to laugh out loud, literally jumped up and down, and clapped her hands while repeating several times, "My mother-in-law made a mistake, my mother-in-law made a mistake!"

Another customer discovered a worn quilt within a tied comforter when she washed and hung the piece on the clothesline. Some of the old quilt showed where the hem in the new covering had come apart. The quilt inside was heavily quilted with a barely visible circular pattern. She drafted the pattern, which featured twenty divisions in a circular sawtooth border around a central star; chose authentic blue, maroon, and cream prints; and stitched a new quilt, re-creating the look of the one made almost a hundred years before. We were unable find the pattern of this quilt in any reference book. Replicating the pattern makes it available to a new generation of quiltmakers.

There are several ways to reproduce a quilt in a larger size than the original. (See

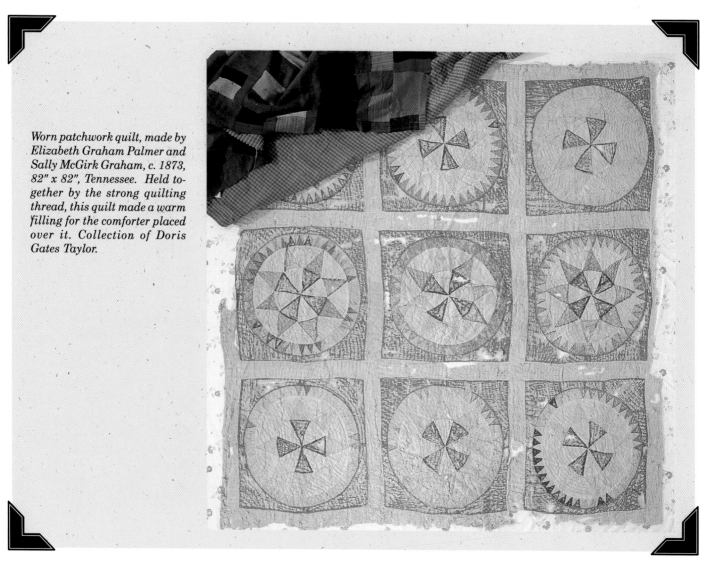

Worn patchwork quilt, made by Elizabeth Graham Palmer and Sally McGirk Graham, c. 1873, 82" x 82", Tennessee. Held together by the strong quilting thread, this quilt made a warm filling for the comforter placed over it. Collection of Doris Gates Taylor.

Four Patch/Tracy's Wedding Quilt on pages 11–12.) Stitching more blocks is the easiest method. Enlarging the blocks is another way. Adding or enlarging the lattice or adding alternate blocks or borders also produces a bigger quilt.

One quickly realizes that replication offers quiltmakers a wide variety of challenges. This book contains guidelines and techniques that I have developed over several years and many quilts. I have provided patterns and sewing instructions for some unusual vintage quilts, along with helpful quiltmaking information. Brief historical notes will help you make knowledgeable decisions about patterns, fabrics, and quilting designs.

Published Reproductions

In *The Romance of the Patchwork Quilt in America,* the book she co-authored in 1935, Rose Kretsinger published her own reproduction quilts, Wreath of Roses and Ohio Rose. She told how she copied the Antique Rose quilt from a quilt fragment left after the 1871 Chicago fire. She copied a nineteenth-century quilt exactly in color and details but added an elaborate border to frame her twentieth-century version, called Pride of Iowa. Her quilts are now in the Spencer Museum of Art in Lawrence, Kansas.[2]

Charlotte Jane Whitehill began making quilts in 1929 in the same Kansas community as Rose Kretsinger. Several of the quilts she made were replicas of family quilts. She was commissioned to reproduce two quilts of rare design from very fragile vintage quilts. In her quilt, pictured in Kretsinger's book, Charlotte Jane Whitehall chose to replicate five blocks of an antique design, Old English Rose, and combined them with four blocks of a contemporary design, Kentucky Rose. She then designed an appliqué border encircling the nine blocks. Many of her quilts are in the Denver Art Museum.[3]

The Stearns and Foster Company acquired finished quilts and printed the patterns for them on the wrappers of their batting. They changed some of the old pattern names. New York Beauty became the new name for Crown of Thorns or Rocky Mountain Road. The quiltmakers or designers were not named on the pattern wrappers, and company records that might reveal more about the quiltmakers were destroyed in the recent reorganization of the company into Stearns Technical Textiles, Inc.

Replicating Vintage Quilts

You can use the basic techniques of quiltmaking to reproduce the antique designs in this book. Some new rotary-cutting and machine-stitching techniques allow you to produce components of the old patterns quickly. See pages 71–83 for a review of general quiltmaking information.

Collecting Patterns

The method you use to obtain patterns from antique quilts (when printed patterns are not available) depends on how the quilt was made.

You can usually draft patchwork patterns with graph paper. Make a sketch of the block or unit for piecing. Measure the block; note the size of center squares or other parts. If necessary, enlist the help of someone who is more comfortable with drafting. Sons and husbands often get very involved in quiltmaking at this stage of "technical" skill.

I drafted graph-paper patterns for several of the replicated quilts in this book. I used the exact measurements for the Log Cabin in Bars Setting (page 25) and for Clara's Quilt/Railroad Crossing (page 43) in transferring the patterns to graph paper. The little squares pieced in the Confetti quilt (page 19) measured about ⅞" in the original quilt. I drafted them 1" square for ease in rotary cutting. Sun and Shade (page 48) was easier to cut and piece with 1¼" half-square triangle units rather than the original 1⅛" units.

Appliqué designs not readily found in printed form can be carefully traced from a vintage quilt. The animal shapes for the child's quilt on page 63 were copied on a copy machine. I then used tracing paper with a permanent transfer pencil to make iron-on patterns. Tracings taken from an appliqué quilt are usually rough sketches and require some refinement.

Butcher paper sometimes helps in planning appliqué quilts that are not sewn in blocks. Draw a half or a quarter of the pattern on the paper with a permanent black pen. If the background fabric chosen for the quilt is light, lightly mark the position of the appliqués on the background fabric over the paper plan. If the background fabric is dark, cut slits in the paper pattern and mark guidelines for the appliqués with a silver or white pencil.

I keep sketches of quilts I see in ball parks and flea markets as well as pictures torn from magazines. I love to "track down" the names of the patterns whenever possible. A small notebook of graph paper is handy for sketching interesting patterns. Please remember to obtain permission to copy the pattern from any quilt that does not belong to you.

Choosing Fabrics

Use the best fabric available for your project. Decide how closely you want to copy the fabrics in the antique quilt. Do you want the same colors, scale of prints, number of prints, and so on? Many reproduction fabrics currently available represent fabrics produced in several different eras. You may find reproduction fabrics nearly identical to those used in your vintage quilt.

According to Jane Nylander in *Fabrics for Historic Buildings,* "A common mistake in replication is to neglect preliminary documentary research. In choosing a reproduction fabric, one should be aware of differences caused by the changing technology of textile production during the past 200 years. In no case can modern commercial spinning and weaving processes duplicate the appearance or texture of hand-production methods, nor can chemical dyes exactly duplicate the colors achieved by vegetable dyes."[4]

Some period fabrics are also available in limited amounts. Print and feedsack yardage from the 1930s is found more often than large pieces of prints from earlier periods. Many times, vintage fabrics are found in pieces that are obviously leftovers from another project. You can determine whether the pieces will be useful if you plan your quilt in advance. (See "Calculating Yardage" on page 10.)

The fabrics used for the replication quilts shown here include different color prints (Lady of the Lake, Hourglass/Time Passes); similar solid colors with very similar print (Animal Friends); vintage 1930s prints with new solid white (Clara's Quilt/Railroad Crossing); all new fabrics (Mosaic #17, Bars and Stars, Four Patch/Tracy's Wedding Quilt); new prints overdyed (Sun and Shade); reproduction prints (Confetti/Criss-Cross); decorator fabrics (Reflection of Eagles); and vintage scraps collected over several years (Barnraising Squares, Log Cabin in Bars, and Hourglass/Time Passes).

Fabric Hunting Hints for Vintage Fabrics

🐦 Check with area quilt shops. Many collect vintage fabrics for quilt restoration. Check with vendors at regional or national quilt shows. Tell them what you need; they may have it at home or may help you find it. Look in local thrift shops (read the clothing labels for fabric content). Go to estate and garage sales. Call up distant relatives who sew. Shop the vintage clothing/costume stores.

🐦 Be patient. It has taken several years to find enough white shirting prints for some of my projects, and I haven't always been able to find long lengths of fabric for borders. One year, I found a set of blue-and-white blocks at a large quilt show.

I promptly set out to find some matching yardage. Not one piece did I find. Lots of black was available that year, however, so I purchased pieces of black. Two years later, I found blue yardage that was perfect for my blocks, along with another set of blocks in black and white!

🐦 Once you have "played" through your own collection looking for the fabric you need, start calling up friends. Start a charm-quilt fabric exchange in your quilting group.

🐦 Quilt shops are currently stocking many reproduction prints. Several companies are printing reproduction fabrics for different time periods, including the 1850s, 1870s, 1890s, 1900s, 1920s, and 1930s.

Calculating Yardage

Once you have planned your reproduction quilt, you must purchase the fabric. Even math-shy individuals can determine fabric requirements by following some simple steps.

1. Make a list by color of the pieces needed.
2. Consider borders and backings first as they require the most fabric.
3. For each piece, determine the number of times it will be cut.
4. For each piece, determine how many times it can be cut across the fabric width.
5. Determine how many rows of the piece are needed.
6. Multiply the number of rows times the measure of the unit.

I find that a sketch of the cutting plan is helpful. Don't forget to buy fabric for binding. A quarter yard of "insurance fabric" is worth every penny.

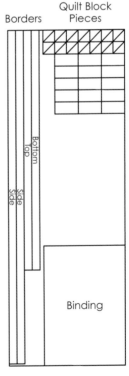

Cutting Diagram

Quilt Patterns

Four Patch/Tracy's Wedding Quilt

My grandmother, Eunice Amanda Descans Hicks, made this quilt and a number of other patchwork quilts in Royal Center, Indiana. She was a member of a quilting club, and several of her quilts, including this one, appear to have been quilted by the group. The fabrics she chose are characteristic of the period in which the quilts were sewn. This one was made about 1905.

Eunice had a high-backed wooden rocking chair, where she pieced her quilts and where I now sometimes piece my quilts. I remember she wore her long white hair twisted into a bun and she taught me nursery rhymes. After my grandmother's death in 1947, my family moved into her house. Over the years, her quilts kept us warm.

When my oldest daughter, Tracy, announced her plans to marry in just nine weeks, I didn't think I

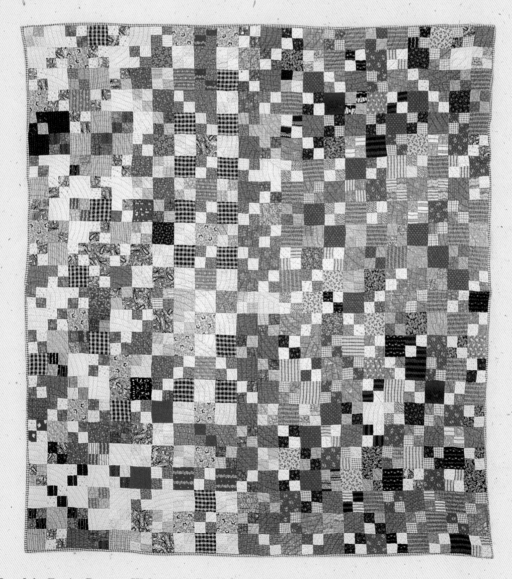

Four Patch by Eunice Descans Hicks, 1905, Royal Center, Indiana. The worn condition of this quilt and its small size were factors in deciding to make a replica: Tracy's Wedding Quilt. (Collection of Sharon L. Hicks Newman)

had time to make her a wedding quilt. She asked if she could have one of my grandmother's quilts and chose the Four Patch. When we got the quilt out of the closet and began to look at it closely, we knew it was too worn for much daily use as well as too small for the king-size water bed the couple was going to use.

My friends in the shop said it was unthinkable for the daughter of a quilt-store owner not to have a wedding quilt. They offered help with the cutting and sewing. Tracy and everyone else in the store enjoyed pulling out bolts of gray, pink, dusty blue, red, and black prints like those in the original quilt. The gingham backing fabric had to be one of a

smaller scale than the original, but with the prints available in 1987, the fabrics for the top were easier to match. When the top was pieced and the fan quilting pattern marked, we put up the quilt frame right in the middle of the shop.

Before the quilting was finished, the staff found it hard to pry me away from the frame, and customers occasionally found themselves cutting fabric, writing out tickets, ringing up sales, and making change. Just before the wedding, we held a luncheon in the shop, attended by staff, family, and my father, Don Hicks, so we could present the replica of his mother's quilt to Tracy.

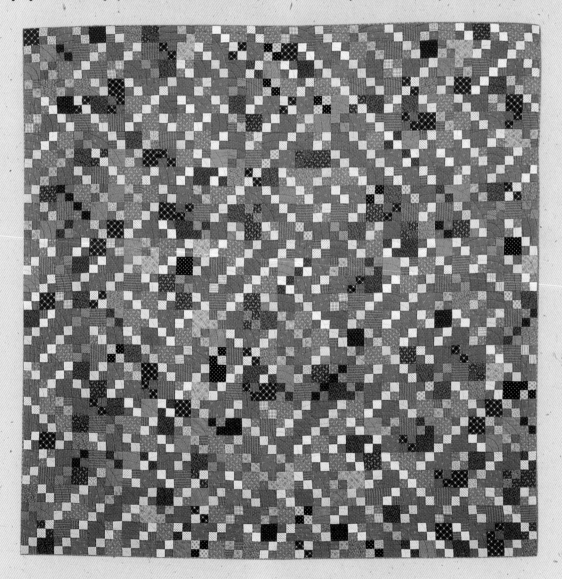

Tracy's Wedding Quilt by Sharon L. Newman and friends, 1987, Lubbock, Texas, 90" x 90". Twenty-eight fabrics were used to replicate the Four Patch quilt in a size to fit a water bed. (Collection of Tracy Newman Faulkner)

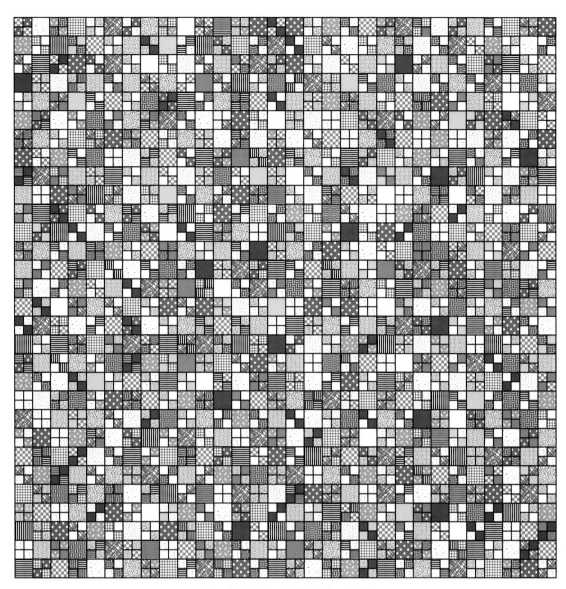

Four Patch/Tracy's Wedding Quilt

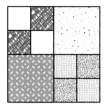

Double Four Patch

Finished Quilt Size: 90" x 90"
Finished Block Size: 6" x 6"
Setting: Straight, side by side

Materials (44"-wide fabric)

2½ yds. (total) assorted light prints for blocks
6½ yds. (total) assorted dark prints for blocks
8¼ yds. for backing and binding
There are 28 fabrics distributed equally
throughout the four quarters of this quilt.

Cutting

From the light prints, cut:

| 43 | strips, each 2" x 42", for four patches |
| 6 | strips, each 3½" x 42", for squares |

From the dark prints, cut:

| 43 | strips, each 2" x 42", for four patches |
| 32 | strips, each 3½" x 42", for squares |

Block Assembly

1. Pair the 2" light and dark strips right sides together, sew, and press the seam toward the dark fabric in each unit.

2. Crosscut into 2"-wide segments.

2"

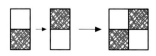

Cut 900 segments (total).

3. For each Four Patch block, sew 2 segments together as shown.

Make 450 Four-Patch units.

4. Crosscut the 3½"-wide light and dark strips into 450 squares, each 3½" x 3½".

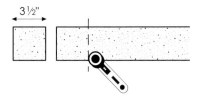

5. Sew a Four Patch to each of the 450 light and dark fabric squares.
6. Sew the Four Patch/square units together in pairs to make double Four Patch blocks.

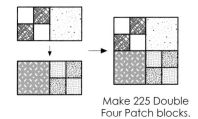

Make 225 Double Four Patch blocks.

Quilt Top Assembly

1. Arrange the blocks side by side, 15 across and 15 down.
2. Sew the blocks together into rows. Press seams of even-numbered rows in one direction, and odd-numbered rows in the other direction.
3. Sew the rows together, matching block seams.

Finishing

Refer to "Quilt-Finishing Techniques" on pages 77–83.

1. Mark the quilting design onto the quilt top. This quilt displays an all-over fan or shell pattern.

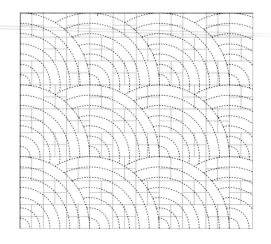

2. Layer the quilt top with batting and backing; baste.
3. Quilt and bind.
4. Sign and date your Four Patch quilt.

History of Quilt Sizes

Quilt sizes have varied considerably throughout the decades. From 1700 to 1830, beds were very large. Often, they were tall so a trundle bed could be stored underneath, and the quilts were made 108" to 144" square to cover both the main bed and the trundle. (That size is appropriate for the king-size beds that enjoy contemporary popularity.) After 1830, bed sizes gradually decreased, and by the mid-1800s, quilts were 78" and 90" square or rectangular.

Quilts from the early 1900s are usually around 80" x 96". Skimpy Depression-era quilts, which utilized about five yards of 36"-wide fabric, reflected the shortages of everything during those years. Typical 1930s quilts measure 72" x 90".

In 1949, Florence Peto addressed the subject of quilt sizes. "There is a practical as well as an aesthetic reason for planning a quilt for the bed on which it is to be used: size. Is there to be a valance around the bed? Are the pillows to be covered by the spread? The manner in which the counterpane is to be used will determine its size, and size will determine the effective disposal of the pieced or appliquéd blocks to be fitted within its margins. Beginners have found it useful to experiment with squares cut from paper which may be placed on the bed to help judge how many blocks of a certain size will be needed and what disposition of them would be most effective; the pattern could be roughly chalked in on one or two of the squares as a further help. A good preliminary plan saves later worry."[5]

Squares All Over/ Barnraising Squares

Displaying a rich catalog of the many fabrics in the quiltmaker's scrap bag, this quilt contains over 360 different fabrics, dating from 1870 to 1900. The quiltmaker repeated more of the dark prints than the light prints. She used many of the light "shirting" prints only once. Perhaps these pieces were samples she obtained for ordering fabrics or ordering shirts. She arranged the fabrics in a sequence of six dark prints and four light prints repeating across the quilt. Then she staggered the rows to form the traditional Barnraising setting. The red prints at the ends of the dark sections, with four regular rows between, unify the wide variety of prints.

This one-patch style of quilt is what I call a "bonus" quilt. As you cut fabric for other quilts, cut a few extra squares. When you have several fabrics cut, sew them into the six dark-print or four light-print units. The squares are easy to sew and make a good take-along travel project. Replicating a quilt with this many different fabrics also helps to justify your stacks of fabric!

When I was preparing to reproduce this scrap quilt, I needed a system for marking the different fabrics. I started along one edge of the quilt and, concentrating on each square, marked each new print with a penny. With 360 different fabrics, this is a $3.60 quilt!

You can piece this quilt little by little, using templates and hand piecing, or rotary cut and piece quickly, following the appropriate set of directions on pages 16–18.

Squares All Over (inset), maker unknown, c. 1900, 88" x 88".

Barnraising Squares *by Sharon L. Newman, 1993, Lubbock, Texas, 88" x 88". This Barnraising setting features more than 360 fabrics. Quilted by The Quilt Shop in 1987. (Collection of Dianna McClendon)*

Squares All Over/Barnraising Squares

Finished Quilt Size: 88" x 88"
Setting: Straight, side by side

Materials (44"-wide fabric)

3½ yds. (total) assorted light prints for units
5 yds. (total) assorted dark prints for units
⅜ yd. red print for units
2⅝ yds. of 108"-wide muslin for backing
⅞ yd. for binding

Template-Cutting Method

From the light and dark prints, cut the
following pieces, using the template on
page 88.

768 light print squares, each 2½" x 2½"
1104 dark print squares, each 2½" x 2½"
64 red print squares, each 2½" x 2½"

Unit Assembly

1. Sew single light-print squares together to make the following units.

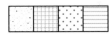

4-square units   3-square units   2-square units
Make 168.   Make 16.   Make 16.

Set aside 16 single light-print squares.

2. Sew dark-print squares and red squares

together to make the following units.

4-square units
Make 24.
Add a red square at each end.

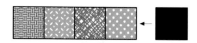

4-square units
Make 8.
Add a red square at one end.

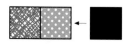

2-square units
Make 8.
Add a red square at one end.

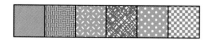

6-square units
Make 120.

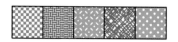

5-square units
Make 12.

4-square units
Make 24.

3-square units   2-square units
Make 12.   Make 16.

Set aside 16 single dark-print squares.
3. See "Quilt Top Assembly and Finishing" on page 18 to assemble these units and finish your quilt.

Rotary-Cutting Method

From the red print, cut:
4 strips, each 2½" x 42". Crosscut the strips into 64 squares, each 2½" x 2½".

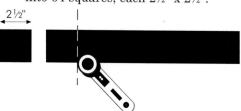

From the assorted light prints, cut:
48 strips, each 2½" x 42". Cut each strip in half crosswise, for a total of 96 strips, each 2½" wide and approximately 21" long.

From the assorted dark prints, cut:
69 strips, each 2½" x 42". Cut each strip in half crosswise for a total of 138 strips, each 2½" wide and approximately 21" long.

Unit Assembly

1. Sew the 2½" x 21" pieces of light prints into 24 panels of 4 strips each, combining the prints randomly.
2. Crosscut the panels into a total of 192 strips, each 2½" wide. Set aside 168 of these strips.

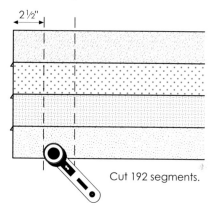

Cut 192 segments.

3. Remove one square from eacn of 16 of the remaining strips.

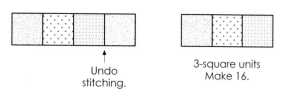

Undo   3-square units
stitching.   Make 16.

4. Divide each of the 8 last remaining strips in half to make 16 two-square units.

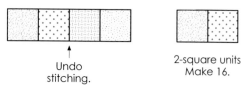

Undo   2-square units
stitching.   Make 16.

5. Sew the 2½" x 21" pieces of dark prints into panels of 6 strips each, combining the prints randomly. Make 23 panels.

6. Crosscut the panels into a total of 184 strips, each 2½" wide. Set aside 120 whole strips.

2½"

Cut 184 segments.

7. Using the remaining strips, remove stitching as required to create the following units.

5-square units
Make 12.

4-square units
Make 48.

3-square units
Make 12.

2-square units
Make 32.

Make 16.

8. Sew a red square to each end of 24 four-square units.
9. Sew a red square to one end of 8 four-square units.
10. Sew a red square to one end of 8 two-square units.

Make 24.

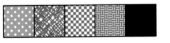

Make 8.

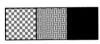

Make 8.

Quilt Top Assembly and Finishing

Refer to "Quilt-Finishing Techniques" on pages 77–83.

1. Arrange the strip units into horizontal rows according to the quilt diagram on page 16.
2. Sew the strip units together into rows. For easier assembly, sew rows together into quarter sections, then join quarter sections to complete the quilt top.
3. Mark the quilting design onto the quilt top. Diagonal lines quilted through the squares create a very traditional look.

4. Layer the quilt top with batting and backing; baste.
5. Quilt and bind.
6. Sign and date your Barnraising quilt.

⊠⊠⊠⊠⊠⊠⊠ **NOTE** ⊠⊠⊠⊠⊠⊠⊠

Use Sally Schneider's scheme for maximizing the mix of prints: "One method for increasing the variety of fabrics in designs pieced with strips is to use just half the length of a strip and double the number of sets required. For example, if a design requires four dark strips and six light strips to be sewn into two sets, you would choose eight half-length dark strips and twelve half-length light strips to make four shorter sets."[6]

⊠⊠⊠⊠⊠⊠⊠⊠⊠⊠⊠⊠⊠⊠⊠⊠⊠⊠

Confetti/Criss-Cross

In this Nancy Page pattern, bits of fabric the size of postage stamps form little Ninepatch blocks framed with more stamp-sized pieces. A chain appears when you alternate the pieced blocks with blocks of muslin.

Perhaps the quiltmaker cut too many little prints and designed the checkerboard border to use them.

This quilt was the first twentieth-century quilt I added to my collection. I was attracted to the quilt by the orderly little squares, a very traditional design.

Close examination revealed the grid of quilting, good workmanship, and the nice border, unusual for a 1930s quilt. When I learned the quilt was made in Vernon, Indiana, my home state, I was sold!

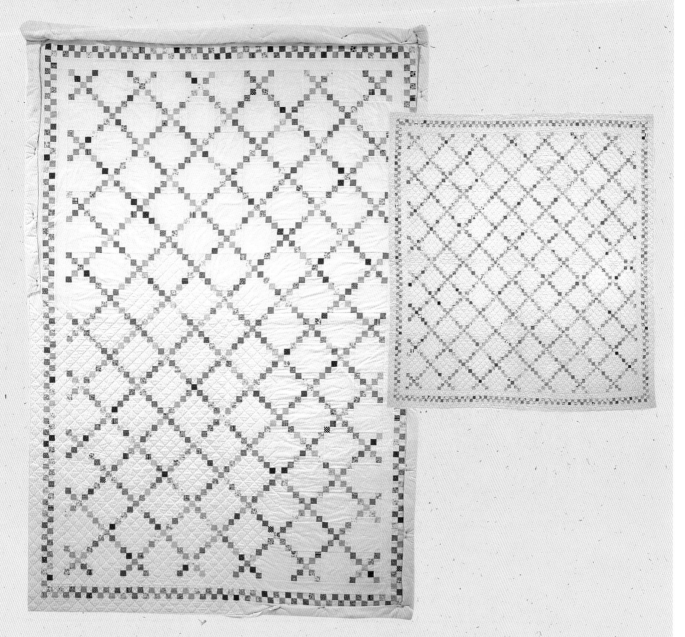

Criss-Cross by Barbara Phiffer, 1993, Shallowater, Texas, 69" x 99". Contemporary prints in this unfinished quilt replicate a postage-stamp quilt from 1930.

Confetti, (inset) maker unknown, c. 1930, Indiana, 73" x 80". Plain blocks alternate with framed Ninepatches, pieced from postage-stamp prints. The blocks are framed with a pieced checkerboard border. (Collection of Sharon L. Newman)

Finished Quilt Sizes:
Wall: 49" x 59"   Double: 79" x 99"
Twin: 69" x 99"   Queen: 89" x 99"
King: 109" x 109"

Finished Block Size: 5" x 5"
Setting: Straight, side by side

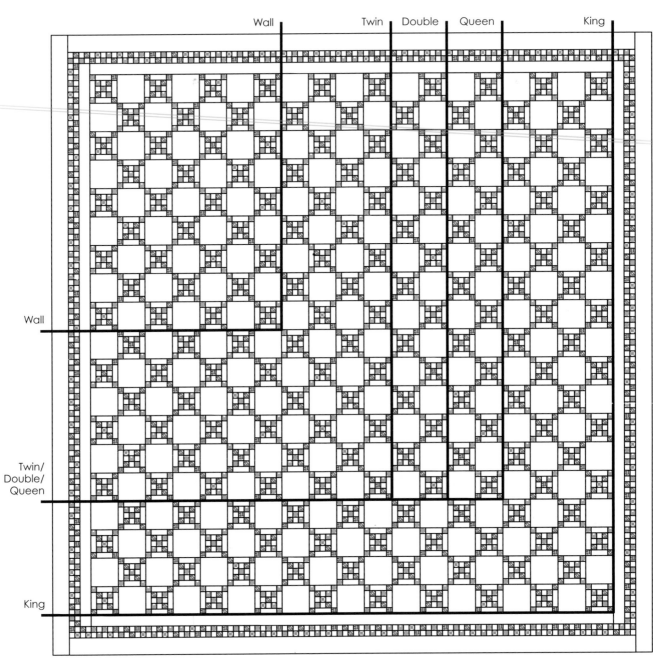

Confetti/Criss-Cross

Materials (44"-wide fabric)

	Wall	Twin	Double	Queen	King
Muslin	3 yds.	6½ yds.	8¾ yds.	10½ yds.	13½ yds.
Assorted prints	1 yd.	2¼ yds.	2½ yds.	2¾ yds.	3½ yds.
Backing	3 yds.	6 yds.	6 yds.	8½ yds.	9½ yds.

Cutting

From the assorted prints, cut the required number of 1½"-wide strips to make the pieced blocks and borders for the quilt size you are making.

Wall	21	Queen	60
Twin	48	King	80
Double	55		

From the muslin, cut the following pieces for the outer borders (OB), inner borders (IB), alternate blocks (AB), pieced blocks (B), and pieced border (PB). Label each set of strips or pieces for easy identification later. Cut in the order given, then cut 2"-wide binding strips from the leftover border fabric. Refer to the cutting diagram. Some pieces require first cuts only; others require two.

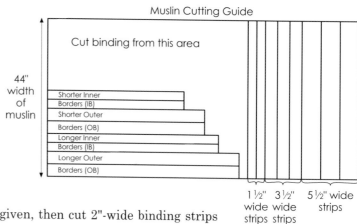

Quilt Size	FIRST CUT		SECOND CUT	
	No. of Strips	Dimensions	No. of Pieces	Dimensions
Wall	2	3½" x 55½" (OB)		
	2	3½" x 45½" (OB)		
	2	2½" x 49½" (IB)		
	2	2½" x 39½" (IB)		
	5	5½" x 42"	31	5½" x 5½"(AB)
	5	3½" x 42"	64	1½" x 3½" (B)*
	17	1½" x 42" (B and PB)		
Twin	2	3½" x 99½" (OB)		
	2	3½" x 69½" (OB)		
	2	2½" x 89½" (IB)		
	2	2½" x 59½" (IB)		
	14	5½" x 42"	93	5½" x 5½" (AB)
	16	3½" x 42"	188	1½" x 3½" (B)*
	36	1½" x 42" (B and PB)		
Double	2	3½" x 99½" (OB)		
	2	3½" x 79½" (OB)		
	2	2½" x 89½" (IB)		
	2	2½" x 69½" (IB)		
	16	5½" x 42"	120	5½" x 5½" (AB)
	18	3½" x 42"	222	1½" x 3½" (B)*
	42	1½" x 42" (B and PB)		
Queen	2	3½" x 99½" (OB)		
	2	3½" x 89½" (OB)		
	2	2½" x 89½" (IB)		
	2	2½" x 79½" (IB)		
	19	5½" x 42"	127	5½" x 5½"(AB)
	20	3½" x 42"	256	1½" x 3½" (B)*
	45	1½" x 42" (B and PB)		
King	2	3½" x 109½" (OB)		
	2	3½" x 109½" (OB)		
	2	2½" x 99½" (IB)		
	2	2½" x 99½" (IB)		
	26	5½" x 42"	180	5½" x 5½"(AB)
	28	3½" x 42"	362	1½" x 3½" (B)*
	61	2½" x 42"		

*Set aside the remaining 3½" strips for step 7 in "Block Assembly" on page 22.

Block Assembly

With each step, make the required number of units and cut the required number of segments for the quilt size you are making.

1. Using the 1½"-wide muslin and assorted print strips, make the required number of three-strip panels (2 print strips with a muslin strip between). Press the seams toward the print strips in each panel.

Wall	3	Queen	10
Twin	8	King	14
Double	9		

2. Crosscut the panels into the required number of 1½"-wide segments.

Wall	64	Queen	256
Twin	188	King	362
Double	222		

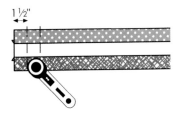

3. Using the remaining 1½"-wide print and muslin strips, assemble the required number of three-strip panels (1 print strip with 2 muslin strips). Press the seams toward the print strip in each panel.

4. Crosscut the panels into the required number of 1½"-wide segments.

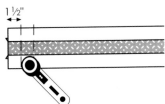

5. Arrange the segments into the required number of Ninepatch blocks indicated at the top of the next column. Sew them together, taking care to match the seams.

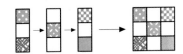

Wall	32 pieced blocks
Twin	94 pieced blocks
Double	111 pieced blocks
Queen	128 pieced blocks
King	181 pieced blocks

6. Sew a 1½" x 3½" muslin strip to opposite sides of each Ninepatch block.

7. Sew 1½"-wide print strips to opposite edges of the remaining 3½"-wide strips of muslin. Press the seams toward the print strips. Make the number of panels required for the quilt size you are making.

Wall	3	Queen	10
Twin	8	King	14
Double	9		

8. Crosscut the required number of 1½"-wide segments from the panels.

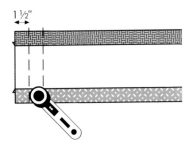

Wall	64	Queen	256
Twin	188	King	362
Double	222		

9. Sew 2 print/muslin/print segments to opposite sides of the Ninepatch blocks.

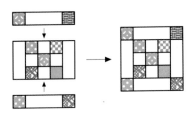

Quilt Top Assembly

1. Beginning the first row with a pieced block, arrange the blocks side by side, alternating pieced blocks and plain muslin blocks. Sew them together into rows, pressing seams toward the pieced blocks.

2. Sew the rows together, matching seams carefully.

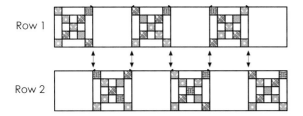

3. Sew the 2½"-wide muslin inner borders first to the top and bottom, then to the sides of the quilt top. (See "Borders with Straight-Cut Corners" on page 77.

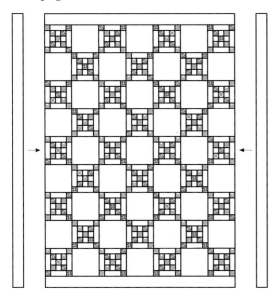

4. For the pieced border, sew 1½"-wide print strips and 1½"-wide muslin strips together into the number of pairs required. Press the seams toward the print strip in each pair.

Wall	7	Queen	15
Twin	12	King	17
Double	14		

5. Crosscut the strips into 1½"-wide segments.

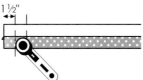

Wall	168	Queen	328
Twin	288	King	388
Double	308		

6. Sew the required number of segments together side by side to form checkerboard border strips.

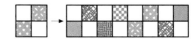

	Top & Bottom Border Strips	Side Border Strips
	No. of Segments	No. of Segments
Wall	35	39
Twin	55	59
Double	65	69
Queen	75	79
King	95	99

7. Sew checkerboard borders, first to the top and bottom of the quilt top, then to the sides.

8. Sew 3½"-wide muslin outer borders first to the top and bottom, then to the sides of the quilt.

Finishing

Refer to "Quilt-Finishing Techniques" on pages 77–83.

1. Mark the quilting design onto the quilt top. The Confetti quilt was quilted in an allover diagonal grid that runs across the blocks and border as shown.
2. Layer the quilt top, batting, and backing; baste.
3. Quilt and bind.
4. Sign and date your Criss-Cross quilt.

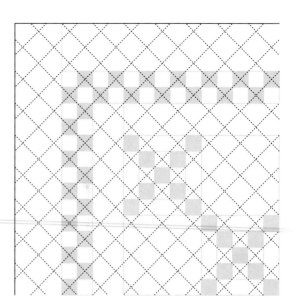

Log Cabin in Bars Setting

Simply arranging the familiar Log Cabin blocks in a diagonal setting produces this unusual "bars" effect. There are only a few recorded examples of this setting, all from the fourth quarter of the nineteenth century.[7]

The maker of this quilt started some blocks with a light fabric piece after the red center, and some with a dark print. She also made a number of blocks with a dark fabric on the wrong side of the block. When she joined the rows, she rotated some of the blocks, an easy mistake to make. The strong color combination is typical of quilts from Pennsylvania, where it was made.

This was a difficult quilt to replicate because I decided first, to match, as exactly as possible, the colors and print styles in the quilt, and second, to sew the blocks and arrange them in the exact same manner, mistakes and all.

To aid in the fabric search, I made a list describing each fabric. This list included the type of printed design (floral, geometric, etc.) and the scale and density of the print. For example, "small viney print of brown and rust on beige" or "widely spaced medium print of tan on olive green."

I kept a written account of what size to cut each fabric, where in the block it was used, and how many times it occurred. One light shirting print occurred in every possible position in the block. A few fabrics appeared only once.

After pulling all possible fabrics from my own collection, I presented the list of fabrics I still required to friends. Everyone knew I wanted a large-scale print with beige on olive green. Even my most trusted sources couldn't find just the right fabric. I made trips to the local thrift shops and found many olive green garments, but not in cotton. Finally, I decided to substitute another color. The fabric I used in place of the hard-to-find olive green was a smaller-scale print in a somewhat darker shade. Some of the scraps I tried, I later rejected for one reason or another. When a sample block didn't have quite the right "tone," I made another.

To re-create the quilt as exactly as possible, I had to individually arrange the pieces of each block before sewing. Once the blocks were assembled correctly, I checked the original quilt for the placement of each block. I spread the original quilt on a guest bed and positioned each new block against the old before sewing them into rows. You may also wish to sew some "mistakes" into some of the blocks of your replica by placing dark fabrics on the light sides of the blocks.

Repeating the color combinations and then copying the arrangement of the blocks gave me a new appreciation for scrap quilts. What a wonderful collection of fabrics that quiltmaker chose! Even with the many prints available in our stores today, our modern quilts don't always have the richness and variety of the vintage scrap quilts.

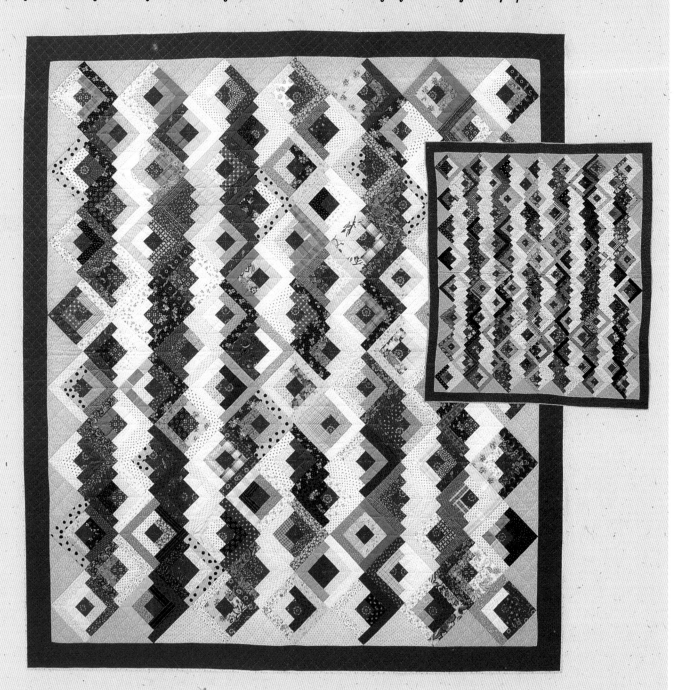

Log Cabin Bars by Sharon L. Newman, 1993, Lubbock, Texas, 75" x 86". The process of re-creating the color and design, piece by piece, in this unusual setting was a challenge.

Log Cabin in Bars Setting (inset), maker unknown, c. 1880, Pennsylvania, 80" x 88". The quiltmaker who set these Log Cabin blocks on the diagonal used many different fabrics and was very casual about the position of the light and dark prints. Medium tones used in both halves of the blocks keep the basic contrast working. (Collection of Sharon L. Newman)

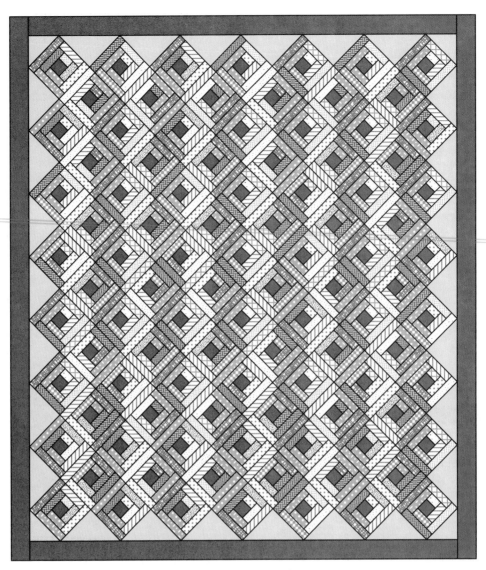

Log Cabin in Bars Setting

Finished Quilt Size: 75" x 86"
Finished Block Size: 7" x 7"
Setting: Diagonal, side by side

Materials (44"-wide fabric)

2½ yds. (total) assorted light prints for blocks
2½ yds. (total) assorted dark prints for blocks
⅔ yd. (total) assorted red prints for block centers
2½ yds. red print for border
1¼ yds. assorted yellow prints for side and
    corner triangles
5½ yds. for backing and binding

Cutting

The pieces for the Log Cabin blocks can be rotary cut to the following dimensions or cut using the templates on page 88.

From the assorted light and dark prints, cut:

98 each of the following "log" sizes for the
    blocks (or use Templates 1–8 on page 88):

#1	1¾" x 2½"
#2, #3	1¾" x 3¾"
#4, #5	1¾" x 5"
#6, #7	1¾" x 6¼"
#8	1¾" x 7½"

From the assorted red prints and red print for border, cut:

98 squares, each 2½" x 2½", for block centers (Template 9)

2 strips, each 3½" x 69½", for top and bottom borders

2 strips, each 3½" x 86½", for side borders

From the assorted yellow prints, cut:

7 squares, each 11¼" x 11¼"; crosscut
twice diagonally into 28 side triangles.
You will use 26.

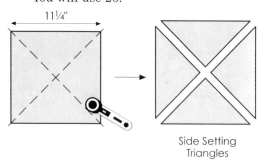

Side Setting
Triangles

2 squares, 5⅞" x 5⅞"; crosscut once diagonally for 4 corner triangles.

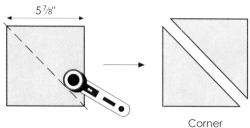

Corner
Triangles

Block Assembly

🌸🌸🌸🌸🌸🌸 **NOTE** 🌸🌸🌸🌸🌸🌸

Although there are faster strip-piecing
methods for making Log Cabin blocks, the
following method is recommended for
making a scrappy Log Cabin like the one
in the photo.

🌸🌸🌸🌸🌸🌸🌸🌸🌸🌸🌸🌸🌸🌸🌸🌸🌸🌸

1. Arrange the pieces for each of the 98
   blocks, following the block diagram
   and referring to the quilt diagram and
   photo for color placement. Begin with
   a light fabric strip for Logs #1 and #2
   in some blocks (Version A) and with a
   dark strip in other blocks (Version B).

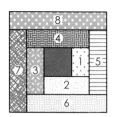

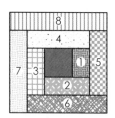

Add logs in
numerical order.
Version A

Version B

2. Sew the logs for each block together
   in numerical order as shown for the
   first 4 logs, always rotating the piece
   a quarter turn in the counterclock-
   wise direction before adding the next
   log. Press the seam away from the
   center square after adding each log.
   Continue until all 8 strips have been
   added to the center square.

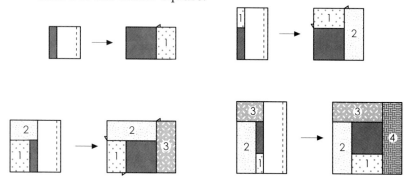

Quilt Top Assembly

1. Referring to the quilt plan (page 26)
   and the quilt photo (page 25), arrange
   the blocks in a diagonal setting, with
   7 blocks across and 8 down. Place the
   blocks in position so that they form
   the "bars" design.
2. Add side triangles and sew the blocks
   together in diagonal rows. Press
   seams in one direction on even-numbered rows and in the other direction
   on odd-numbered rows. See "Diagonal Settings" on pages 75–76.
3. Sew corner triangles to the corners
   last.
4. Referring to "Borders with Straight-
   Cut Corners" on page 77, measure
   and sew borders to the top and bottom of the quilt. Then add borders to
   the sides.

Finishing

Refer to "Quilt-Finishing Techniques"
on pages 77–83.

1. Mark the quilting design onto the
   quilt top. The blocks in this quilt were
   quilted with an X, then a +, then a box
   that joins the tips of the +. The side
   triangles and the corners were quilted
   with a grid dividing their outside edges

in fourths. The border is quilted with diagonal grid lines 1" apart.

2. Layer the quilt top with batting and backing; baste.
3. Quilt and bind.
4. Sign and date your Log Cabin in Bars Setting quilt

❦❦❦❦❦❦❦ **NOTE** ❦❦❦❦❦❦❦

On the original Log Cabin quilt, the backing was pulled to the front of the quilt and hemmed for a self binding.

❦❦❦❦❦❦❦❦❦❦❦❦❦❦❦❦❦❦❦

Patriotic Quilts

Whenever patriotism is intensified by national anniversaries or armed conflicts, quiltmakers gather red, white, and blue fabrics together. With patriotic inspiration, quilters design and create one-of-a-kind arrangements of stripes, stars, flags, eagles, and blocks reminiscent of flags, expressing their personal patriotic sentiments in bold graphics. There are many good examples of quilts with patriotic themes because such quilts are generally well cared for by the families in which they were made.

Textile manufacturers must plan ahead in order to produce fabrics at the appropriate time for wartime commemorations and other significant dates. For example, several fabric designs were inspired by the recent anniversary of Columbus's discovery of the New World.

Bars and Stars

This quilt was hanging in the front window of a little shop in Colorado, and I walked right past it, intent on seeing another quilt displayed across the room. After completing the tour of all the quilts in the store, I returned to this one and read the tag as the pattern name would not come to mind. I left the store, looking back at the quilt in the window. It really had sparkle. The next day, I returned and purchased the quilt.

The block pattern is New Waterwheel, a design published in the 1930s in Nancy Cabot, a syndicated column written by Loretta Leitner Rising for the Chicago Tribune.[8]

The red, white, and blue colors are compatible with quilts made during the First World War, and the size, setting, and amount of quilting are consistent with other patriotic quilts of that era. The distinctive cadet blue print is another strong clue that this is a quilt from the first quarter of the twentieth century.

This pattern is perfect for beginning quiltmakers. New rotary-cutting and machine-piecing shortcuts make quick work of the Ninepatch center. The "bar" units are easy to strip-piece and crosscut to the proper size. The corner squares are also easy to sew using the Bias Square technique. Setting the pieced blocks diagonally with alternate blocks creates the stars and makes the quilt sparkle.

Bar and Stars by Sharon L. Newman, 1993, Lubbock, Texas, 63" x 76". The dynamics of a red, white, and blue combination remain strong in this last decade of the twentieth century.

Bars and Stars (inset), maker unknown, c. 1918, Indiana, 70" x 82". Red, white, and blue blocks in a diagonal setting form crisp blue stars between small Ninepatches. (Collection of Sharon L. Newman)

Finished Quilt Sizes:
Wall: 38¼" x 51"   Double: 76" x 89¼"
Twin: 63" x 76"   Queen: 89¼" x 102"
King: 102" x 114¾"

Finished Block Size: 9" x 9"
Setting: Diagonal, side by side

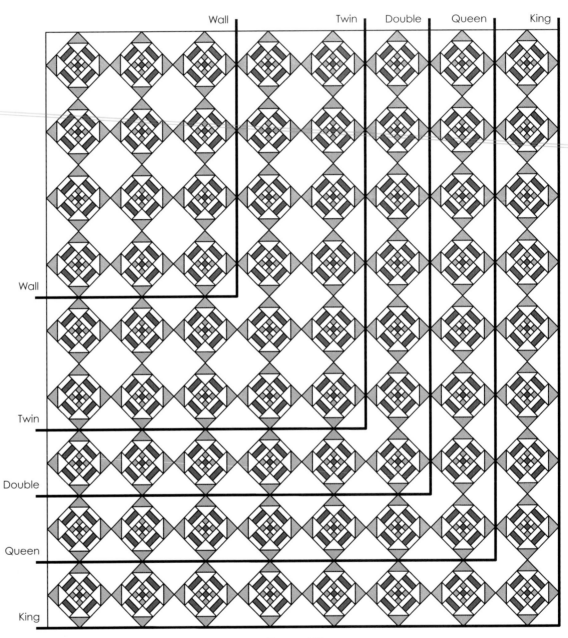

Bars and Stars

Materials (44"-wide fabric)

	Wall	Twin	Double	Queen	King
White Solid	2½ yds.	5½ yds.	6½ yds.	9½ yds.	11½ yds.
Red Solid	⅓ yd.	⅔ yd.	1 yd.	1¼ yds.	1½ yds.
Blue Solid	¾ yd.	1½ yds.	1¾ yds.	2 yds.	2½ yds.
Backing	1⅝ yds.	5 yds.	5⅓ yds.	8 yds.	9⅓ yds.
Binding	½ yd.	¾ yd.	¾ yd.	⅞ yd.	1 yd.

From each of the 3 fabrics, cut the required number of 1½" x 42" strips for the quilt size you are making.

Fabric	Wall	Twin	Double	Queen	King
Blue	2	6	8	10	12
Red	5	13	18	24	30
White	11	29	40	53	66

From the remaining white fabric, cut the required number of the following pieces:

Piece	Wall	Twin	Double	Queen	King
9½" Squares for Alternate Blocks	6	20	30	42	56
14" Squares* for Side Setting Triangles	3 / 10	5 / 18	6 / 22	7 / 26	8 / 30
7¼" Squares** for Corner Setting Triangles	2	2	2	2	2

*Cut the 14" squares twice diagonally for the required number of side setting triangles.
**Cut the 7¼" squares once diagonally for 4 corner setting triangles.

Cutting Half-Square Triangle Units

Using the remaining blue solid and white solid fabrics, follow the directions for "Making Half-Square Triangle Units" on pages 72–73 to make the required number of triangle units.

Wall	Twin	Double	Queen	King
48	120	168	224	288

Block Assembly

For each step, make the number of units and cut the number of segments required for the quilt size you are making.

1. Sew together 1½"-wide strips into panels of white/red/white. Press the seams toward the red strip in each panel.

Wall	Twin	Double	Queen	King
5	13	18	24	30

2. Crosscut the required number of 1½"-wide segments from the panels.

Wall	Twin	Double	Queen	King
12	30	42	56	72

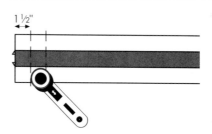

3. For the bar segments of the block, also crosscut the required number of 3½"-wide segments from the panels.

Wall	Twin	Double	Queen	King
48	120	168	224	288

4. Assemble the required number of panels of 1½"-wide blue and white strips. Press the seams toward the blue strips.

Wall	Twin	Double	Queen	King
1	3	4	5	6

5. Crosscut the panels into 1½"-wide segments.

Wall	Twin	Double	Queen	King
24	60	84	112	144

1½"

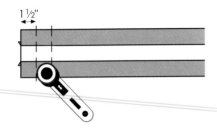

6. For each block, sew 1½"-wide segments into Ninepatch blocks with red at the center.

7. Sew a half-square triangle unit to each end of a 3½"-wide white-red-white segment, positioning the units as shown.

Make 2 for each block.

8. Sew a 3½"-wide white-red-white segment to opposite sides of each of the center ninepatch units as shown.

Make 1 for each block.

9. Assemble the 3 rows into a Ninepatch block. Make the number of blocks required for your quilt.

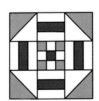

Wall	12 pieced blocks
Twin	24 pieced blocks
Double	36 pieced blocks
Queen	49 pieced blocks
King	64 pieced blocks

Quilt Top Assembly

1. Referring to the quilt plan, arrange the pieced blocks into diagonal rows with the alternate blocks and the side and corner triangles.
2. Sew the blocks together, pressing seams in even and odd rows in opposite directions. See "Diagonal Settings" on pages 75–76.
3. Sew the rows together, taking care to match the seams between the blocks and easing if necessary.

Finishing

Refer to "Quilt-Finishing Techniques" on pages 77–83.

1. Mark the quilting design onto the quilt top. Quilt alternate blocks in diagonal lines 1½" apart to form diamonds. Quilt the pieced blocks "by the piece" (¼" away from seams), with diagonal lines over the white squares in the center Ninepatch.

2. Layer backing, batting, and quilt top; baste.
3. Quilt and bind.
4. Sign and date your Bars and Stars quilt.

Fabric Technology

At the end of the nineteenth century, widespread changes in the design and production of textiles in England, France, Germany, and Austria resulted in the manufacture of larger quantities of textiles from many designers and workshops. One firm, the Weiner Werkstatte (WW), founded in 1903, produced textiles by more than eighty designers between 1905 and 1923. Records show the incredible output of textile patterns during this period by some of the WW textile workshop designers: Hoffmann, 6,204; Moser, 330; Kitty and Felice Rex, 76, and Dagobert Peche, 1,766.[9]

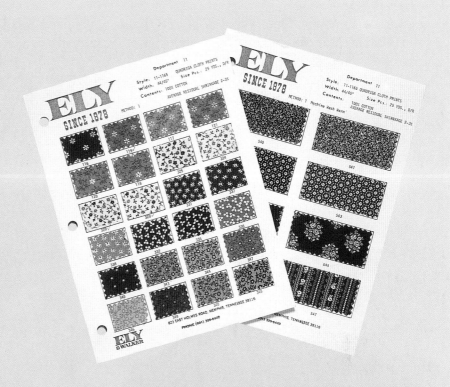

The American textile industry was also producing large quantities of fabric by the end of the nineteenth century. By 1880, American manufacturers had the capacity to produce 800,000,000 yards of printed textiles a year, enough for each woman and girl in the country to have seventeen new dresses.[10]

American fabrics were moderate to low priced as the industry continued to increase production for the fast-growing American mass market. Many print works added over 1000 new fabric patterns each year. Most sold for less than 10 cents a yard. Manufacturing and marketing of fashion fabrics increased. Rapid changes in the styles of women's clothing kept pace with increased fabric production. Women could buy from an amazing variety and quality of domestic and imported goods. Choices included prints and solids, checks, plaids, dots, and stripes as well as floral designs. Well-stocked department stores offered fabrics at all price levels. The finer, more expensive fabrics were still imported from Europe.

Mail-order catalogs offered both fashion and decorator fabrics. Availability of factory-produced household linens, children's clothing, and men's shirts increased, but most women's clothing continued to be sewn at home.

Even Texas frontier homemakers could purchase the new dress patterns by mail and receive the latest fashion news from magazines, such as *Godey's Lady's Book and Magazine, Peterson's Magazine,* or *Harper's Bazaar.*

"The cut of all the late nineteenth-century dress styles created leftover fabric scraps. Since women continually updated their wardrobes, they accumulated a variety of scraps. The Victorian crazy quilts showcased the finer fabrics of the times, as well as the quiltmaker's skilled needlework. Thrifty and practical women used dressmaking scraps in pieced quilt block designs, even though they could purchase inexpensive fabric."[11]

Evidence of the different dress fabrics incorporated into quilts can be found in the Log Cabin quilts of the late nineteenth century. In addition to the Log Cabin quilts made of cotton prints, there are many that were made with silk or wool sewn and pressed onto foundations, both in the traditional settings and the Pineapple variation.

Around 1900, American industry met the increasing demand for textiles by producing cheaper, lower-quality goods using new printing technologies. Textile manufacturers produced millions of yards of low-thread-count greige (pronounced "gray") goods, printed in the most inexpensive manner. Simple stripes, geometrics, and floral designs of a single color—usually pink, gray, red, maroon, blue, brown, or black—were printed on a white background. These fabrics of simple design worked well in men's clothing—hence the name shirting prints. Reverse prints, with white on a colored background, were achieved by discharge printing (bleaching) on already-dyed fabric.

Recently, textile companies have printed reproduction fabrics with colored backgrounds in large quantities. However, very few white backgrounds are printed with the look of the old shirting prints desired by many quiltmakers.

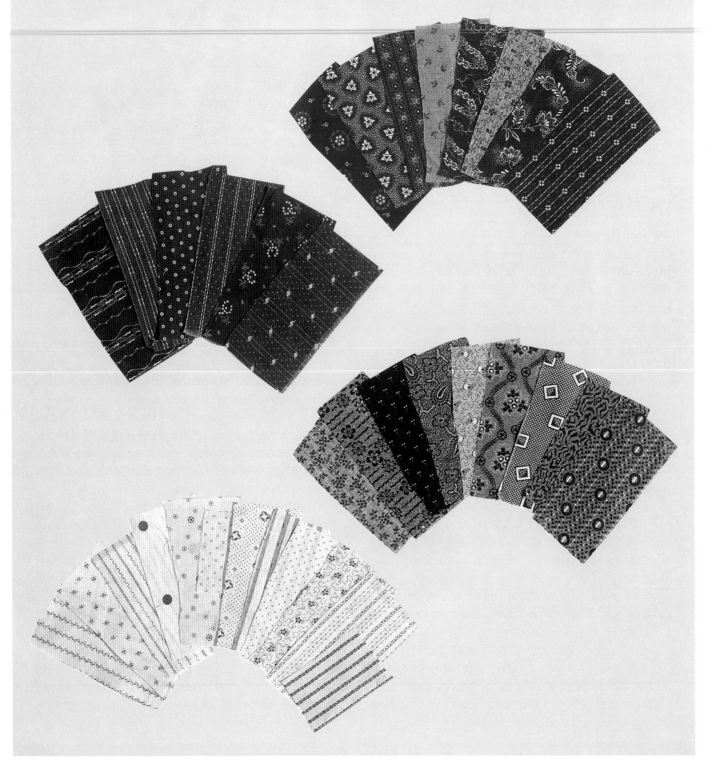

Mosaic #17

A square divided into two triangles is a basic unit for many of the patchwork patterns sewn since the eighteenth century. Several hundred patterns can be formed by using contrasting fabrics in the triangles, rotating the squares, and arranging them in grids of four, nine, sixteen, or twenty-five.

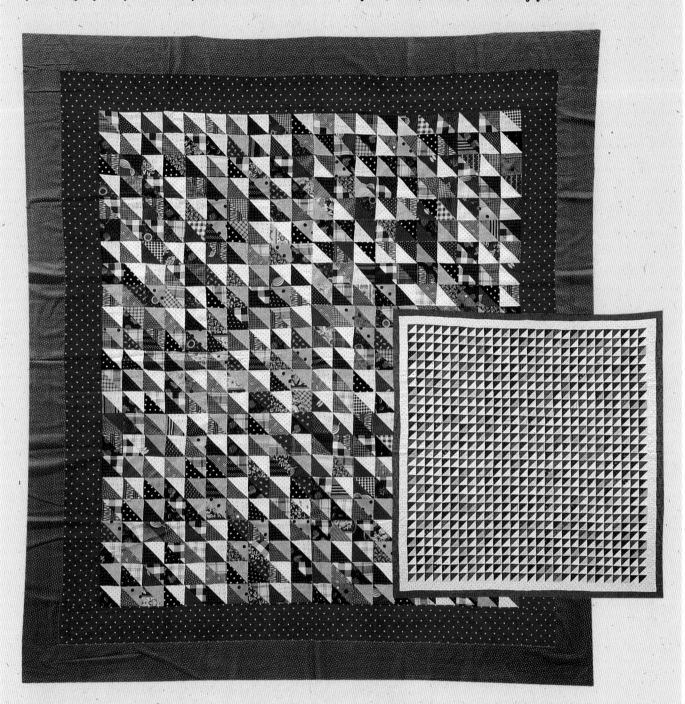

Mosaic #17, *unquilted top, maker unknown, 1875–1900, 85" x 97". A rich variety of colors and prints, framed with red and green, showcases the quiltmaker's "palette." (Collection of Sharon L. Newman)*

Mosaic #17, *(inset) maker unknown, c. 1900, 75" x 78". A sampling of the many shirting prints and the broad variety of blue and white prints in this quilt provide a visual record of the very distinct changes in the fabric-production industry at the turn of the century. (Collection of Sharon L. Newman)*

In the quilt top shown in the large photo on page 35, the quiltmaker arranged fabrics at random, using a variety of fabrics both in color and scale of pattern. Some green and yellow-with-black prints were from Ely and Walker, a textile manufacturer that printed distinctive calico patterns from 1878 to 1984. Some early shirting prints were also incuded. Both woven and printed ginghams were used, and they were not always cut on the straight grain of the fabric. Note the many polka-dot prints: a large brown dot on tan, a medium white dot on black, and a tiny black on red. Several colors and sizes of leaf prints were also included.

The unknown Iowa quiltmaker who stitched the quilt on page 35 used thirty-six different dark blue prints and twenty-eight different light prints. Although the colors are predominantly navy and white, the multiple shades of navy mix well with the variety of early shirting prints. A sprinkling of light triangles of a narrow red stripe and a few with a tiny lavender gingham warm the cool blues. The graphic straight-line prints and windowpane checks occur in multiple sizes. The largest windowpane print pulls the eye across the surface of the quilt.

Black with white prints, white with black prints, gray prints with black or white—all have been my favorites for a long time. I have acquired many little bits of fabric and stored them for years. When my shop promoted charm quilts with patterns and fabric-exchange sessions, quilting friends contributed to my black-and-white collection.

I like to study old scrap quilts for a system of organization. Sometimes a single color will be the unifying factor, sometimes a repeated fabric. Most quilts show some organization. All three examples of Mosaic #17, however, are randomly arranged. Because I tend to overcoordinate most of my projects, I was determined to let this one happen randomly. I pieced the 812 half-square triangle units required for this quilt at random by cutting strips from every black, white, or gray fabric in my collection. I sewed bias panels, alternating dark and light but sometimes substituting one of the grays in either position. As I completed the first few squares, the overall appearance was disappointing, but as I made more squares and arranged them into a small project, the contrasts got better, and I was encouraged to complete the remainder of the squares. I stacked all the squares in a box, set it up by the sewing machine, and sewed four-square-by-four-square blocks without matching. Then I sewed these together randomly. After several unsuccessful attempts to use a double border of white and black, I finally chose the tiny white stripe on black for the border.

Mosaic #17 by Sharon L. Newman, 1993, Lubbock, Texas, 78" x 80". Black, white, and gray prints, collected over many years, combine to create this stunning quilt.

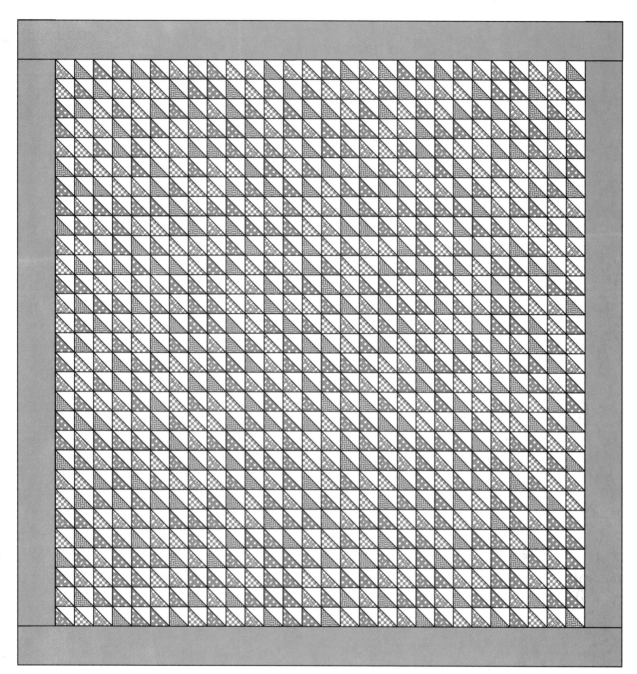

Mosaic #17

Finished Quilt Size: 78" x 80"
Finished Block Size: 2½" x 2½"
Setting: Straight, side by side

Materials (44"-wide fabric)

3 yds. (total) assorted light prints for blocks
3 yds. (total) assorted dark prints for blocks
2½ yds. dark print for border and binding
5½ yds. for backing

Cutting

From the dark print for border, cut:
2 strips, each 4½" x 78½", for top and
   bottom borders
2 strips, each 4½" x 81", for side borders

Block Assembly

1. Referring to "Making Half-Square
   Triangle Units" on pages 72–73,
   make 812 dark/light half-square triangle units, each 3" x 3", from the assorted light and dark prints.

2. Sew half-square tri-
angle units together
into blocks of 16
squares.

Make 42.

3. Sew the remaining
half-square triangle
units into blocks of
20 squares, with 4
squares across and 5
squares down.

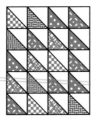

Make 7.

Quilt Top Assembly

1. Arrange the 16-square blocks into 6
horizontal rows of 7.
2. Add the 7 larger blocks for the final
horizontal row.
3. Referring to "Borders with Straight-
Cut Corners" on page 77, attach border strips to the sides of the quilt top.
Then add top and bottom borders.

Finishing

Refer to "Quilt-Finishing Techniques"
on pages 77–83.

1. Mark the quilting design onto the
quilt top. The grid for quilting this
pattern is drawn off-center.

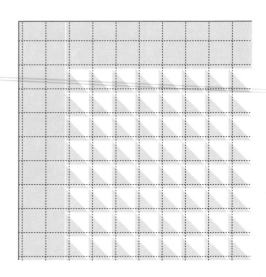

2. Layer the quilt top with batting and
backing; baste.
3. Quilt and bind.
4. Sign and date your Mosaic #17 quilt.

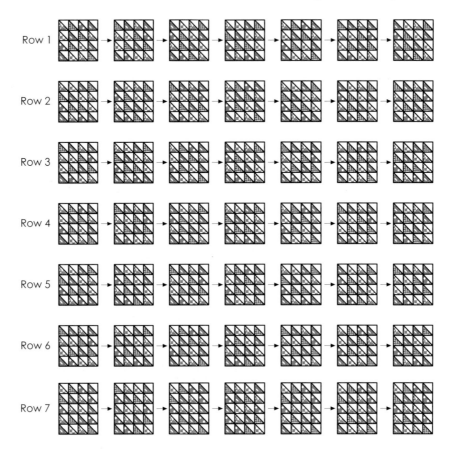

Row 1 → → → → → →

Row 2 → → → → → →

Row 3 → → → → → →

Row 4 → → → → → →

Row 5 → → → → → →

Row 6 → → → → → →

Row 7 → → → → → →

Bar Codes for Quilts?

The patchwork striped design on the back of the black-and-white half-square Mosaic Quilt #17 is one of my unfinished projects now completed. I pieced the Universal Pricing Code in reaction to the new merchandising technology entering my quilt shop. A salesman had spent considerable time explaining that his company's scanner would make ordering much faster and more accurate. All the notions and books soon would be marked with the little black-and-white rectangular codes. When the store opened in 1979, there weren't many sources in existence for quilt patterns or books, and the notions suppliers had only a few items especially for quilters. The need for my homey little shop to leap into the modern technology of 1986 was somewhat disconcerting to me.

During the next week, while I was analyzing the wisdom of signing on with the scanner company, I presented a program on antique quilts in a nearby town. During the lunch hour, I checked out the local fabric store and spied some black-and-white striped fabrics. The sight of these fabrics, and the notion in the back of my mind that quilting for me had come to only mean pricing, inspired the black-and-white bar code design. The stripes made the project easy to sew, but a suitable backing and a quilting design were postponed in deference to more pressing projects.

As I progressed on the black, white, and gray half-squares for the Mosaic quilt, the bar code quilt top came to mind. I coded the numbering to reflect the year the shop opened, the year the bar code was pieced, and the year the project was completed. The "Q" is for quilt, of course. The piece was too long for the quilt top and so I turned it diagonally. The fabrics I used to fill out the corners are some leftovers from the top. The pattern of black-and-white roses I collected in the garment district of New York on a vacation.

"Back art" is the term used by quiltmakers to describe the designs on the back sides of their contemporary quilts. The practice is not new, however, as country quilters with limited funds often pieced together scraps for two tops and quilted them with whatever filling they could afford.

Quilting Designs by Marie Webster

Several of my Indiana quilts, including an 1860s Ninepatch, a late 1890s Star, my grandmother's "V" quilt, and "Clara's Quilt" (page 43) are quilted in double or triple lines. Two lines of quilting lie barely ¼" apart, then a space about 1" wide is unquilted, then the double rows repeat. I have questioned quilters in other areas of the country and found that the double and triple quilting lines seem less common elsewhere than in Indiana and surrounding states, although some are found in all geographical areas.

From the 1990 edition of *Quilts: Their Story and How to Make Them,* I learned more about quilts made in northern Indiana, where the author, Marie Webster, lived. She presented programs about quilting to women's groups in a broad area around her hometown of Marion. Her book included her observations about the older quilts she had studied. Some of the quilts

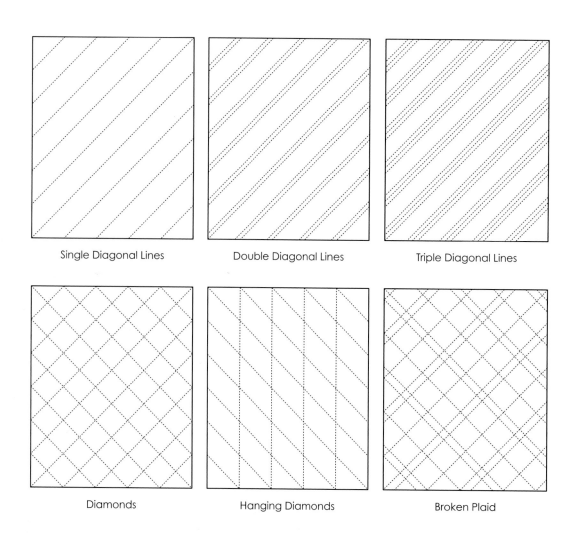

Single Diagonal Lines   Double Diagonal Lines   Triple Diagonal Lines

Diamonds   Hanging Diamonds   Broken Plaid

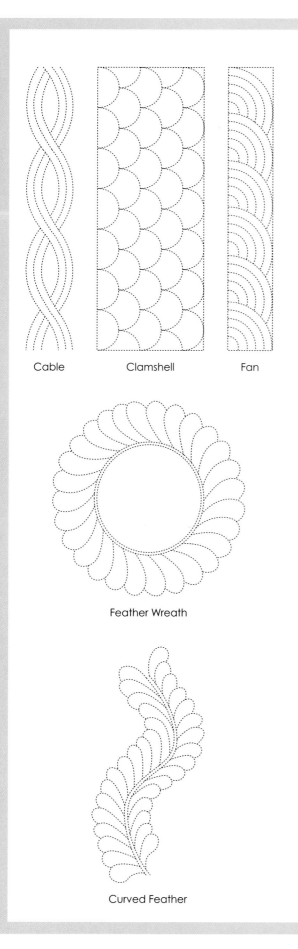

Cable   Clamshell   Fan

Feather Wreath

Curved Feather

she made and showed during her programs have the double and triple diagonal lines of quilting. In her book, originally published in 1915, she discussed the quilting designs found on Indiana quilts made in the early part of the 1900s.

"Patterns of quilting are not as plentiful as designs for the patchwork tops of quilts; only about eight or ten standard patterns being in general use. The simplest pattern consists of 'single diagonal' lines spaced to suit the work in hand. The lines run diagonally across the quilt instead of parallel with the weave, in order that they may show to better advantage, and also because the cloth is less apt to tear or pull apart than if the quilting lines are run in the same direction as the threads of the fabric. The elaboration of the 'single' diagonal into sets of two or more parallel lines, thus forming the 'double' and 'triple' diagonals, is the first step toward ornamentation in quilting. A further advance is made when the quilting lines are crossed, by means of which patterns like the 'square, 'diamond,' and 'hanging diamond' are produced.

"Wavy lines and various arrangements of hoops, circles, and segments of circles are among the more complex quilting patterns which are not particularly difficult. Plates and saucers of various diameters are always available to serve as markers in laying out such designs. The 'pineapple', 'broken plaid,' and 'shell' patterns are very popular, especially with those who are more experienced in the art. One very effective design used by many quilters is known as the 'Ostrich Feather.' These so-called feathers are arranged in straight bands, waved lines, or circles, and—when the work is well done—are very beautiful. The 'fan' and 'twisted rope' patterns are familiar to the older quilters but are not much used at the present time."[12]

Making Quilts by Hand or Machine

The earliest quilts were sewn entirely by hand, as were all family clothing and household linens.

The first breakthrough in the development of a sewing machine was moving the eye of the needle from the top (as in hand sewing needles) to the point. From the first sewing machine patent in 1790, inventors made numerous attempts to develop a workable machine. Walter Hunt made several improvements on the first crude machines but did not patent them. Elias Howe did record the machine he made in 1846. It carried thread in a shuttle below the needle, and a moveable arm created a lock stitch. In 1854, A. B. Wilson introduced the automatic feed.

Isaac Merritt Singer, working as a mechanical repairman, improved the design of a sewing machine brought in for repair, and so impressed his employer that he was given time to perfect his design. His first machines were put into production and sold before they were even patented.

With financial and legal help, Singer withstood the "sewing machine wars," when the filing of many patent-infringement suits threatened to destroy the industry. Settlement resulted in the formation of the "Sewing Machine Combination" with Howe, Singer, and two other manufacturers.

The influence of the sewing machine affected home, factory, and industry, and therefore high finance. Advertising promoted the new machines, and demonstrators in elaborate showrooms showed how easy they were to use. Machine names included "Iron Needle Woman" and "Common Sense Family Sewing Machine." One machine was aptly named "Domestic." Singer promoted the "Merry Singer." Sales escalated when Singer initiated a "hire for purchase plan." A woman could take home and use a $100 machine for a $5.00 down payment and a guarantee to pay the rest at $3.00 per month.

Before 1860, a total of 130,000 machines were sold. In 1876, the total was 262,316 machines sold for the year. A quilting attachment was invented in 1892.

Machine topstitched bindings are sometimes found on quilts with extensive handwork. To emphasize that she had the economic wherewithal to own a machine, a quilter would often use white thread to machine quilt over her patchwork of colors. Men also liked to experiment with the machines.

In general, sewing machines were used more for the everyday sewing tasks, such as making clothing, draperies, and linens, giving women more time to hand quilt their quilts.

Women sewed more pieced quilts by machine than appliqué quilts. Some topstitched their appliqué quilts, but not until the 1960s did the satin stitch increase the amount of machine appliqué.

Whether to machine quilt a new quilt copied from an old one is a personal choice for the quiltmaker. Most vintage quilt tops and blocks, however, will not tolerate machine quilting. The durability and strength that make machine stitching desirable in clothing are more than some older quilt fabrics can withstand.

Clara's Quilt/Railroad Crossing

I was attracted to this quilt by the strong geometry of the white lattice and the use of red to unify the hundreds of little print triangles. The pattern name is Railroad Crossing. Examples of this pattern from the early 1920s can be found in several Amish quilts made in Indiana and Ohio,[13] but this version using Depression-era prints is unusual.

Closer inspection revealed the mirror-imaged nature of the large triangles. Double lines of quilting slant across the lattice and, embroidered in one

Railroad Crossing by Sharon L. Newman, 1993, Lubbock, Texas, 71" x 71". Vintage thirties' fabrics replicate an unusual quilt from 1936.

Clara's Quilt (inset), maker unknown, 1936, 80" x 80". Embroidered on a corner: "Mother, Clara, 1936." Note the unifying effect of the strong red triangles over the multicolored, more pastel triangles. (Collection of Sharon L. Newman)

corner, is: "Mother, Clara, 1936." This is another great Indiana quilt, the second 1930s quilt I added to my collection.

I used authentic 1930s prints with new, bleached muslin to replicate "Clara's Quilt." The challenge of this design was duplicating the mirror-imaged pieced triangle units with prints of similar color and scale. Quick piecing with the Bias Square technique (see pages 72–73) made the pattern's 2,048 individual triangles less intimidating.

Double lines of quilting slant across the lattice, and the lines quilted across the triangles take the path with the least amount of seam allowance to quilt through—a lesson from a quiltmaker of a previous generation!

Clara's Quilt/Railroad Crossing

Finished Quilt Size: 75" x 75"
Finished Block Size: 14⅛" x 14⅛"
Setting: Straight, with lattice

Materials (44"-wide fabric)

6 yds. white fabric for background
4 yds. (total) assorted prints for half-square triangle units and triangles
½ yd. (total) assorted red prints for half-square triangle units and triangles
4½ yds. for backing
¾ yd. for binding

Cutting

From the white fabric, cut:
- 12 lattice strips, each 3½" x 14⅝"
- 3 lattice strips, each 3½" x 66"
- 16 strips, using the template on the pullout pattern
- 2 strips, each 4" x 65½", for top and bottom borders
- 2 strips, each 4" x 75½", for side borders
- 2"-wide bias strips for half-square triangle units

From the assorted prints, cut:
- 2"-wide bias strips for half-square triangle units
- 96 squares, each 2⅜" x 2⅜"*

From the assorted red prints, cut:
- 2"-wide bias strips for half-square triangle units
- 32 squares, each 2⅜" x 2⅜"*

*Crosscut once diagonally.

Block Assembly

1. Referring to "Making Half-Square Triangle Units" on pages 72–73, sew together white and print bias strips and cut 896 half-square triangle units, each 2" x 2".

2. For each pieced block, arrange half-square triangle units in rows of 7, 6, 5, 4, 3, 2, and 1 to form 2 large triangles as shown. Place a unit with a red print at the outside corner of each large triangle. Add triangles to complete the rows, using red triangles in the two remaining corners. Make 2 mirror-image triangles for each block.

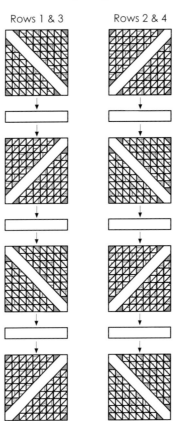

7 6 5 4 3 2 1

3. Sew the half-square triangle units and small triangles together in vertical rows, pressing the seams in one direction for the odd-numbered rows and in the opposite direction for the even-numbered rows. Sew the rows together to complete each triangle, taking care to match seams.

4. To complete each block, sew a large pieced triangle to each side of a diagonal strip. Press the seams toward the pieced triangles. Make 16 blocks.

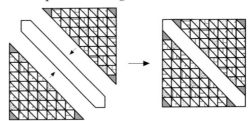

Quilt Top Assembly

1. Arrange blocks in 4 vertical rows of 4 blocks each, with 3½" x 14⅝" lattice strips between them. Sew the blocks and lattice strips together into rows.

Rows 1 & 3   Rows 2 & 4

2. Referring to the quilt plan on page 44, arrange the rows with 3½" x 66" lattice strips between them. Sew rows and lattice strips together.

3. Sew the border strips to the top and bottom of the quilt, then to the sides, as shown for "Borders with Straight-Cut Corners" on page 77.

Finishing

Refer to "Quilt-Finishing Techniques" on pages 77–83.

1. Mark the quilting design onto the quilt top. Straight lines of quilting run through the diagonal rows of triangles. Sets of double diagonal lines ¼" apart with 1" between them fill the diagonal lattice strips and border.

2. Layer the quilt top with batting and backing; baste.

3. Quilt and bind. (Cut a straight-grain binding from the leftover border fabric.)

4. Sign and date your Railroad Crossing quilt. Please provide more information than "Mother, Clara, 1936" so future generations will know something about you and your quilt.

▩▩▩▩▩▩▩ **NOTE** ▩▩▩▩▩▩▩

To enlarge this quilt, make the half-square triangle units larger. Adjust the lengths of the lattice, diagonal strips, joining strips, and borders to correspond with the larger units. Half-square triangle units that are 2" finished will produce a quilt 89" square, including 4" borders. Ones that are 2½" finished will produce a quilt 105" square, including 4" borders.

▩▩▩▩▩▩▩▩▩▩▩▩▩▩▩▩▩▩▩▩

Indigo

Indigo blue dye was in continuous use from earliest textile dyeing records through 1873, when Levi Strauss introduced the first Double X Blue Denim 501's, until the end of the nineteenth century when a synthetic product "indixyl" was developed and began to take its place. Although the process of making indigo dye is complicated, the lumps of dye produced were often used as a medium of exchange—a color as good as gold!

The superiority of indigo rests on its non-fugitive characteristic, so that goods dyed with it do not fade, and that it is what dyers call a substantive dye or fermentation-bath dye—the only one the vegetable kingdom has to offer. It dyes both vegetable and animal fibers with results that cannot be achieved, even approximately, with any other vegetable dye.[14]

Eliza Lucas Pinckney spent her life promoting the development of indigo as a South Carolina export crop. The cultivation of indigo was not easy. The soil had to be carefully prepared, and once the bushes began to grow, they had to be watched carefully until the crucial moment, just before blooming, when the leaves were ready to cut. The leaves were then steeped in water in large vats open to the sun until they fermented and turned the water a greenish color, a process that could take several days. Teams of men, directed by an indigo maker who never left the premises, observed the process both day and night. When the indigo maker decided the process was complete, the solution was strained and poured into a second vat along with a small amount of limewater, where it was beaten with paddles until it began to thicken. This agitation determined the final color of the dye; the longer the mixture was beaten, the darker the color became. Finally, the solution was put into a third vat and allowed to settle before the clear water was drawn off, leaving a sediment that was formed into dye cakes. After the cakes were carefully dried in the shade, they were ready for market.[15]

Every dye works, big or little, had to have two separate areas. One area had to be larger for "colour" dyeing, with all the many vats and vessels required, and for dyeing with substantive dyes of different kinds. The other was a smaller, though perhaps more important, area called the "blueing room," where fermentation-vat dyeing with indigo was carried out. The distinctive color difference between the blues of the 1880s and the blues after 1900 marks the transition to the artificial dye that earned its discoverer, Adolph von Baeyer, the Nobel prize in 1905.

Twentieth-century navy blue printed fabrics have mostly been produced with a synthetic indigo dye, although Japanese and South African textile producers continue to dye with true indigo.

Sun and Shade

Two-color quilts were common during most of the nineteenth century. This indigo-and-tan design is particularly graphic. The distinctive fruity smell associated with indigo dye still lingers on these dark prints.[16] While sun and shade are necessary for the production of indigo dye, the origin of the pattern name is not recorded.

Sun and Shade by Sharon L. Newman, 1993, Lubbock, Texas, 70" x 90". A collection of navy blue prints overdyed with tan replicates the antique quilt well, even though reproductions of the dark indigo prints are difficult to obtain.

Sun and Shade (inset), maker unknown, c. 1890, Texas, 66" x 80". The deep, dark indigo prints indicate a quilt top pieced some years before the striped lining and ties were used to complete the project. (Collection of Eleanor Bartholomew)

The pale blue-striped backing fabric on this quilt is several years newer than the fabrics in the quilt top. Quite often, an unfinished quilt top is layered with batting and tied years after it was pieced. This piece is in good condition. The batting has not separated, even though it is sparsely connected by the ties.

The navy blue and dark blue prints in the replicated quilt, a Nancy Page pattern, are all recent. They were originally navy blue with white-print details. In order to replicate the aged appearance of the earlier Sun and Shade quilt, these fabrics were overdyed with tan Rit dye. I chose not to dye the prints with tea, although tea dyeing dates to the era of the Baltimore Album quilts in the 1840s and 50s.

Crib   Double   Queen/King

Crib

Double

Queen/
King

Sun and Shade

Finished Quilt Size:
Crib: 40" x 60"   Double: 70" x 90"
Queen/King: 90" x 110"

Finished Block Size: 10"
Setting: Straight, side by side

Materials (44"-wide fabric)

	Crib	Double	Queen/King
Navy Blue Prints (assorted ½-yd. pieces)	3 yds.	8 yds.	12½ yds.
Tan Solid	3 yds.	9 yds.	11 yds.
Backing	1¾ yds.	5⅓ yds.	8 yds.
Binding	½ yd.	¾ yd.	1 yd.

Cutting

Refer to the cutting guide to make best use of the ½-yard pieces of navy blue print.

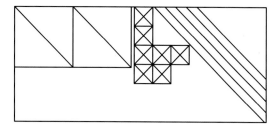

Cutting guide for ½-yard pieces of navy blue print

From both the navy blue prints and the tan solid, cut:
The required number of squares 9⅝" x 9⅝", then cut each diagonally into 2 triangles.

Crib	12
Double	32
Queen/King	50

From each navy blue print, cut:
4 bias strips, each 1¾" x 42"
7 squares, each 3" x 3"; cut each square twice diagonally for a total of 28 triangles.

From the tan solid, cut:
4 bias strips, each 1¾" x 42"
7 squares, each 3" x 3"; cut each square twice diagonally for a total of 28 triangles.

Block Assembly

When assembling the blocks, note that the half-square triangle units in the pieced bands that join the large navy blue print and tan triangles match the print in the navy blue triangle.

1. Referring to "Making Half-Square Triangle Units" on pages 72–73, pair tan and navy blue print bias strips to make bias-strip panels and cut 8 half-square triangle units, 1¾" x 1¾", for each navy blue triangle.

Make 8
for each block.

2. Sew 1 small navy blue print triangle to 1 half-square triangle unit for each block (Unit A).

Unit A

3. Sew both a tan and a navy blue print small triangle to a half-square triangle unit (Unit B). Make 6 for each block.

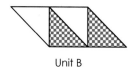

Unit B

4. Sew 1 tan triangle to 1 half-square triangle unit for each block (Unit C).

Unit C
Make 1 for
each block.

5. For each block, arrange 1 Unit A, 6 Unit B, and 1 Unit C as shown and sew the units together.

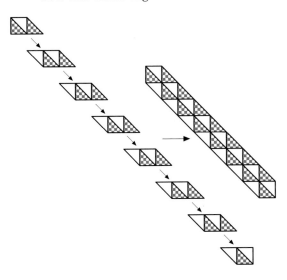

6. Sew a large navy blue print triangle to the light side of the patchwork strip for each block. Take care not to stretch the bias side of the triangle. Press the seam toward the navy blue triangle. Sew a large tan triangle to the dark side of the patchwork strip for each block. Take care not to stretch the bias side of the triangle. Press the seam toward the tan triangle.

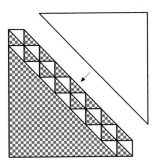

Quilt Top Assembly and Finishing

Refer to "Quilt-Finishing Techniques" on pages 77–83.

1. Referring to the quilt plan, arrange the blocks, rotating the position of the navy blue triangle to form the pinwheel-like overall pattern.
2. Mark the quilting design onto the quilt top. A four-petal curved design was overlaid on the intersecting corners of the tan and navy blue triangles. Straight lines were quilted through the centers of the half-square triangle units and around the edges of the blocks.

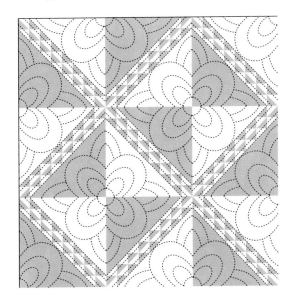

3. Layer the quilt top with batting and backing; baste.
4. Quilt and bind.
5. Sign and date your Sun and Shade quilt.

Tying Quilt Tops

Both the original Hourglass and the Sun and Shade quilts shown in this book are tied rather than quilted.

Victorian Crazy quilts are often found with ties connecting the elaborately stitched top to a backing. The construction method for Crazy quilts, where odd-shaped pieces were stitched on a fabric foundation, created a heavy top that was difficult to quilt. Other foundation-style quilt patterns, such as Log Cabin and Pineapple, are often found with ties. Many of these were made in the third quarter of the nineteenth century, and the ties were not usually very distinctive.

Sewing thread or perle cotton was used like a tailor's tack to connect the heavy top layer with the backing. After 1900, yarn ties were used more often and usually created significant holes in the fabric.

Another motivation for tying a project, rather than quilting it, was to get a warm covering ready in a short time. Often a patchwork top was tied over a worn quilt or old blanket to save time and materials. Generally, tied pieces show more wear sooner than quilted pieces. Rather than tying a vintage quilt top, if you don't wish to or have the time to quilt it, consider leaving it for a quilter in a future generation.

Ursula's Circle

In 1873, Ursula Palmer Garner and her husband, William Lewis, left Tennessee for Texas. They were given a quilt to take along. It was made by Ursula's mother, Elizabeth Graham Palmer, and her grandmother, Sarah (Sally) McGirk Graham. The quilt received hard use and, near the turn of the century, was recycled as the filling for a comforter, pieced and tied by Ursula or her daughter. Ursula's personal clothing, a quilt top, and this comforter were left to daughter Fannie Bell Garner Gates when Ursula died in 1909.

Doris Gates Taylor found the patchwork comforter in a box stored on her mother's farm. She washed and hung it on the line to dry. The blue wool yarn ties came apart and Doris could see the filling was a patchwork quilt. She removed the patchwork of dark, menswear fabrics and uncovered a very worn nine-block quilt. Doris brought the pieces of the comforter to my shop for consultation. Because of the very heavy quilting in the patchwork quilt, enough fabric remained that colors were discernible. I recommended to Doris that she make a replica of this family piece.

This is Doris Gates Taylor's first quilt. She drafted the pattern from the very worn family quilt and stitched a new quilt, re-creating the look of the one made more than one hundred years before. Doris even hand carded cotton that was grown on the family farm and used it as batting in her quilt. She quilted on her mother's quilting frame and posed for photographs wearing a long-sleeved blouse that had belonged to her grandmother.

This is an unknown pattern. It does not appear in any of the usual reference books. By replicating the pattern, Doris has preserved it for another generation of quiltmakers.

Ursula's Circle, *(above), by Doris Gates Taylor, 1986, O'Donnell, Texas, 82" x 82". Replicated from the worn family quilt (right) found in a comforter (see also page 7).*

Ursula's Circle

Finished Quilt Size: 82" x 82"
Finished Block Size: 23" x 23"
Setting: Straight, with lattice

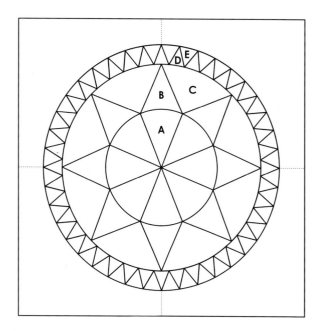

Materials (44"-wide fabric)

2½ yds. light print for lattice and binding
3 yds. black print for background
1 yd. blue print for outer star circle
4 yds. assorted light, medium, and dark
  prints for circle centers
5 yds. for backing
½ yd. for binding

Cutting

From the light print for lattice, cut:

2 strips, each 4" x 75½", for top and
   bottom borders
2 strips, each 4" x 82½", for side borders
2 strips, each 3½" x 75½", for long lattice
6 strips, each 3½" x 23½", for short lattice

From the black print, cut:

9 background squares, each 23½" x 23½"

From the blue print, cut:

72 star points, using Template B on page 86

From the assorted light, medium, and dark prints, cut:

72 light and dark wedges for the star cen-
    ter, using Template A on page 86
72 light or medium wedges for the star
    center, using Template C on page 87
360 wedges for the blue print outer ring,
     using Template E on page 87
360 medium and dark star points using Tem-
     plate D on page 87

Block Assembly

1. Sew together 4 pairs of Piece A for
    each of the 9 circle blocks. Sew the
    pairs together into half circles.

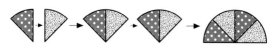

2. Join the half circles to make 9 com-
    plete circles.

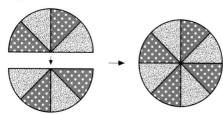

3. Sew together 8 pairs of Piece B and Piece C for each block. Sew the pairs together to make a complete circle.

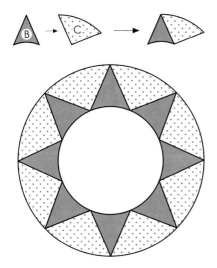

4. Pin the outer edge of the star center to the inner edge of the star-point circle, right sides together, matching seam intersections as shown in the block diagram on page 54. Sew them together, easing as necessary, or use the following appliqué technique.

Make a freezer-paper appliqué template for each of the center circles. Iron a circle template to the back of each center circle. Appliqué the circles to the centers of the star-point pieces (B and C). Remove the freezer-paper template.

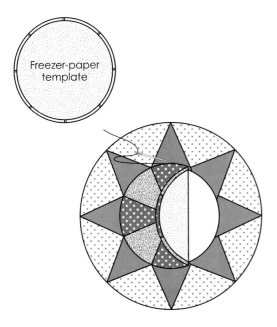

5. Sew together 40 pairs of Piece D and Piece E for each block. Sew the pairs together to make a complete circle.

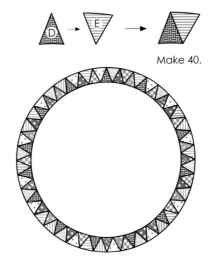

Make 40.

6. Pin the outer edge of the center star to the star-point circle, right sides together, matching points as shown in the block diagram on page 54. Sew them together, easing as necessary, or use the following appliqué technique.

Make a freezer-paper appliqué template the finished size of the star-point circle for each block. Iron the freezer-paper templates to the backs of the center circles. Appliqué the center circle to the outer circle of points, lining up points of large and small stars at the quarter-circle points as shown.

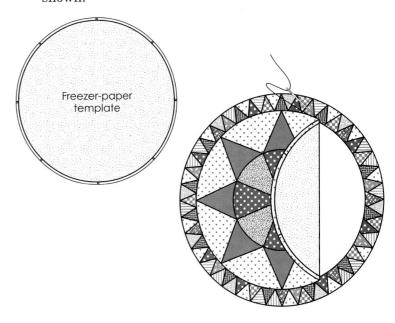

7. Fold background blocks in half twice. Press lightly and mark the center of the block and the centers of each side.

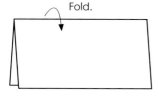

Fold.

Fold again.

Mark center and centers of sides.

8. Make freezer-paper templates the fin-ished size of the outer star-point circle for each block. Iron them to the backs of the circles and pin the circles in place on the background squares, lining up the star points with the center marks on each side of the squares. Appliqué the circles to the back-ground squares.

Cut away the back-ground fabric behind each circle, leaving a ¼"-wide seam allowance. Remove the freezer paper.

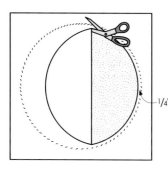

¼"

Quilt Top Assembly

1. Arrange the blocks in 3 rows of 3 blocks with 3½" x 23½" lattice strips between them. Sew the blocks and lat-tice strips together in rows.

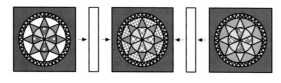

2. Arrange the rows with 3½" x 75½" lattice strips between them. Sew to-gether the rows and lattice strips.

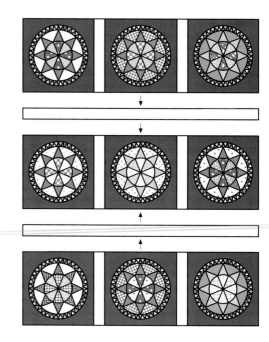

3. Add border strips to the top and bot-tom of the quilt, then to the sides. Refer to "Borders with Straight-Cut Corners" on page 77.

Finishing

Refer to "Quilt-Finishing Techniques" on pages 77–83.

1. Mark the quilting design onto the quilt top. The original quilt was quilted with a shell design with stitching lines ⅝" apart. The replica was quilted "by the piece" in the star, with hearts fill-ing the star background.

2. Layer the quilt top with batting and backing; baste.
3. Quilt and bind.
4. Sign and date your Ursula's Circle quilt.

Hourglass/Time Passes

Tiny triangles that require the smallest scraps are charming in this yard-square child's quilt. Ruth Finley called the simple four triangles-in-a-square pattern Yankee Puzzle. Another common name for this pattern is Envelope.

The soft brown and pink prints are interspersed with red and navy blue prints. The batting is very thin, and the piece has not been quilted; instead, red yarn ties anchor the corners of the squares.

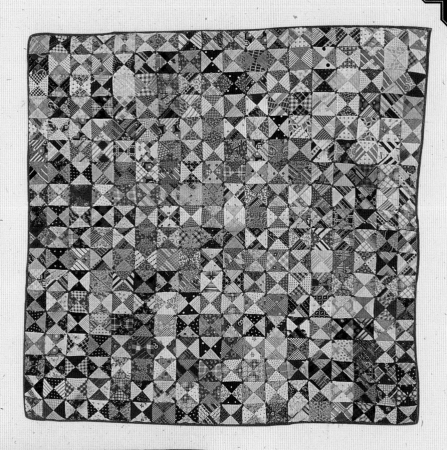

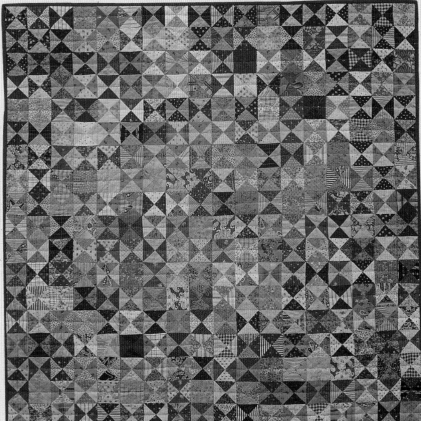

Hourglass (above), maker unknown, 1850–75, 36" x 36". Tiny scraps provide a catalog of the fabrics available to the quiltmaker. (Collection of Sharon L. Newman)

Time Passes (left) by Sharon Newman, 1994, Lubbock, Texas, 36" x 36". Another catalog of quiltmaking scraps.

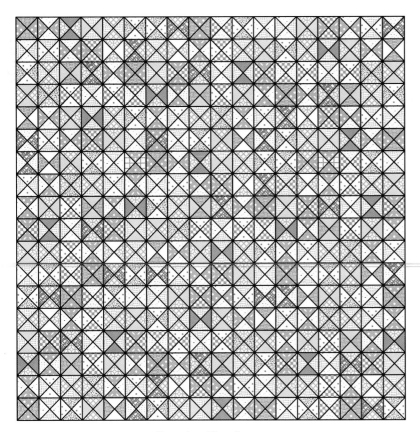

Hourglass/Time Passes

Make 162 of these half-triangle units.

Draw a diagonal line
and stitch 1/4" on each side.

Cut squares apart.

Open and press seam
toward dark triangle.

2. Pair 2 half-triangle units with right sides together and colors reversed. Mark a diagonal line across the seam and sew the squares together, stitching 1/4" away on either side of the marked line. Cut apart on the marked line. Make 324 of these units.

Mark diagonal across the seam and stitch 1/4" away on each side.

Cut squares apart on marked line.

Open and press
seams to one side.

Quilt Top Assembly and Finishing

Refer to "Quilt-Finishing Techniques" on page 77–83.

1. Referring to the quilt plan, arrange the Hourglass blocks in 18 rows of 18 blocks. Alternate the position of the dark prints. Sew the blocks together into rows, pressing the seams in the odd-numbered rows in one direction and the seams of the even-numbered rows in the opposite direction.

2. Sew the rows together, taking care to match the seams between the blocks.

3. Mark the quilting design of your choice onto the quilt top.

4. Layer the quilt top with batting and backing; baste.

5. Quilt and bind or tie.

6. Sign and date your Hourglass quilt.

Finished Quilt Size: 36" x 36"
Finished Block Size: 2" x 2"
Setting: Straight, side by side

Materials (44"-wide fabric)

1½ yds. assorted dark prints for blocks
1½ yds. assorted light prints for blocks
1¼ yds. for backing
½ yd. for binding

Cutting

From the dark prints, cut:
    162 squares, each 3¼" x 3¼"
From the light prints, cut:
    162 squares, each 3¼" x 3¼"

Block Assembly

1. Pair a light square and a dark square with right sides together. Draw a line from corner to corner on the wrong side of the light square. Sew the squares together, stitching 1/4" away on either side of the marked line. Cut apart on the marked line. Press the seam toward the dark triangle.

Basket Lattice/Reflection of the Past

This small quilt top was sent to me with quilt blocks, pieces, and fabric scraps from the estate of Florence Kistler, a family acquaintance who lived in Royal Center, Indiana. Sometimes quilt pieces from the past surprise us. The color graphics of this quilt seem very modern. The diagonal development of the pattern begins with several different blue prints, circa 1900. Then the prints change to designs and colors more typical of the 1920s and 1930s.

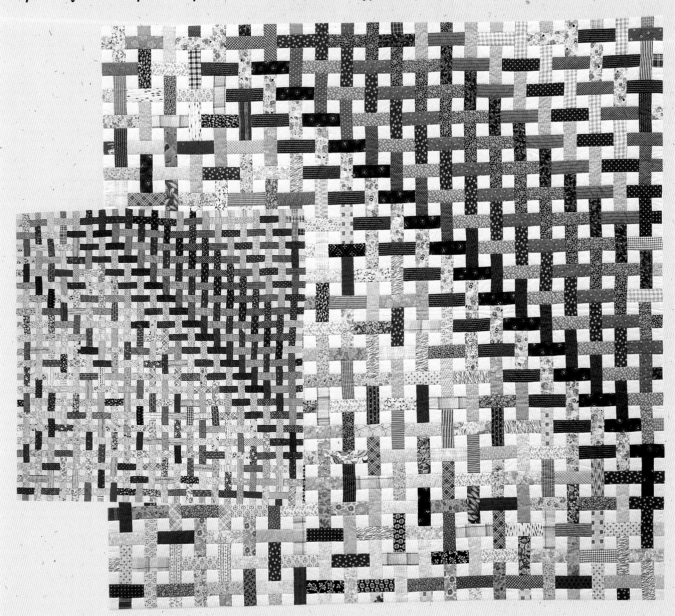

Reflection of the Past by Sharon L. Newman, 1994, Lubbock, Texas, 67½" x 67½". This quilt is a replica of a strikingly modern 1930s quilt top.

Basket Lattice (inset), circa 1930, quiltmaker unknown, Indiana, 67" x 67". The fabrics in this unusual quilt top suggest that it was probably made by two generations of quiltmakers.

Basket Lattice/Reflection of the Past

Finished Quilt Size: 67½" x 67½"

Materials (44"-wide fabric)

1⅔ yds. cream solid for background
2½ yds. (total) assorted light and dark prints
    for lattice
4 yds. for backing
½ yd. for binding

Cutting

From the cream solid, cut:
529   squares, each 2" x 2"

From the assorted prints, cut:
 44   squares, each 2" x 2"
242   rectangles, each 2" x 5"

Quilt Top Assembly

1. Refer to the photo and the quilt plan to determine the positioning of light and dark prints. Begin the first row by joining 1 print square to 2 background squares as shown. Press seams toward the print square.

2. Add a print rectangle to form Unit A. Press the seam toward the rectangle. Make 11 for Row 1.

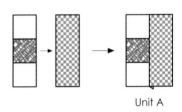

Unit A

3. To make Unit B, partially sew a background fabric square to each long side of a print rectangle. Sew a little more than half of the seam. Sew 11 for each row.

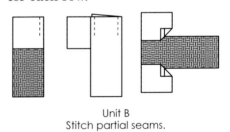

Unit B
Stitch partial seams.

4. Sew Unit B to Unit A.

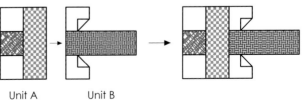

Unit A   Unit B

5. Complete Row 1 by sewing print rectangles between the 11 A/B Units.

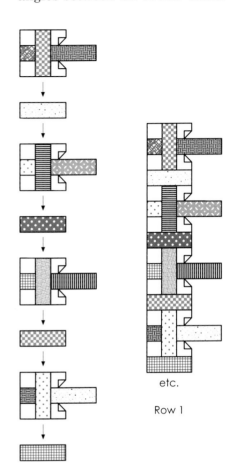

etc.

Row 1

6. For Row 2, make 11 B units and add a print rectangle to each to form the C units.

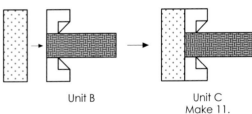

Unit B   Unit C
                          Make 11.

7. To add Unit C to Row 1, first sew the long edge of the print rectangle to the row. Then complete each of the partial seams.

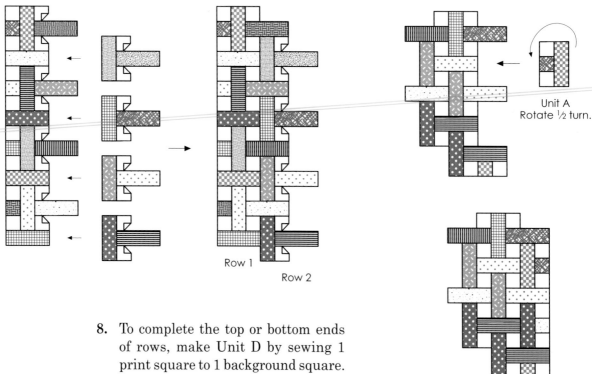

Row 1

Row 2

10. For the final row, make 11 A units, rotate them 180°, and sew them into the gaps of the previous row.

Unit A
Rotate ½ turn.

8. To complete the top or bottom ends of rows, make Unit D by sewing 1 print square to 1 background square. Add Unit D by sewing the print square to the partially sewn square, then complete the seam along the long side of the print rectangle.

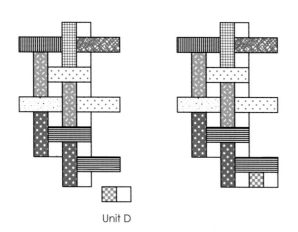

Unit D

9. Continue making and adding Unit C in the gaps of the previous rows to complete 11 rows.

Finishing

Refer to "Quilt-Finishing Techniques" on pages 77–83.

1. Mark the quilting design onto the quilt top. This quilt was quilted in-the-ditch around the squares and rectangles.
2. Layer the quilt top with batting and backing; baste.
3. Quilt and bind.
4. Sign and date your Basket Lattice quilt.

Animal Friends

Baby quilts are often the most worn of family quilts. However, this one, purchased in an antique shop in Carlsbad, New Mexico, appears to have never been washed. Patchwork blocks for crib quilts are typically small. Four- to seven-inch versions of traditional patterns are common. Every style and nearly every pattern has been used in baby quilts.[17]

Appliqués may depict familiar nursery rhymes or children's activities. Many crib quilts are one-of-a-kind designs because the maker personalized the quilt for the child receiving it. The folk-art appliqués of childhood objects, toys, puppy dogs, or storybook characters are rarely found as printed patterns. The animals appliquéd on this little quilt are similar to the coloring-book pictures widely available before television super heroes changed the style of coloring books. The crib quilt I made for my oldest daughter, Tracy, was designed from a coloring book of children's toys purchased for five cents in Austin, Texas, in 1963.

Animal Friends (above), maker unknown, c. 1920. Buttonhole stitches outline coloring-book style animals with simple embroidery details. (Collection of Sharon L. Newman)

Animal Friends (left) by Sharon L. Newman, 1993, Lubbock, Texas, 30" x 50". Pastel green and yellow blocks with simple animal shapes make an endearing baby quilt, which was stitched just in time for a second grandchild.

Animal Friends

Cutting

From the yellow solid, cut:

  7 squares, each 11½" x 11½"

From the green solid, cut:

  8 squares, each 11½" x 11½"

From the print, cut:

  7 animal shapes, using the templates on page 89–95.

Quilt Top Assembly

1. Trace the animal shapes and the flower design for embroidery onto tracing paper with a hot-iron transfer pencil. (Templates are printed so that the transfer will produce the same orientation for the animals as shown.)

Draw animal shapes with transfer pencil.

2. Position animal transfers, tracing side down, on the right side of the print fabric, allowing at least ½" between figures for seam allowances. Press with a hot iron. Position flower designs on the centers of the green blocks and press with a hot iron.

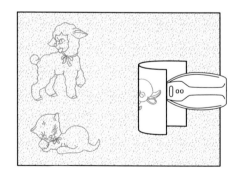

Finished Quilt Size: 33" x 55"
Finished Block Size: 11" x 11"
Setting: Straight, side by side

Materials (44"-wide fabric)

3 yds. yellow solid for blocks and backing

1¼ yds. green solid for blocks

⅔ yd. print for appliqués

½ yd. for binding

Embroidery floss in green, yellow, red, black and colors to match the print fabric for appliqués

Hot-iron transfer pencil

3. Embroider flowers on the green blocks in yellow with double lazy daisy stitch. Stitch stems with green chain stitches and use lazy daisy stitches on the leaves. Make a brown French knot at the flower center.

4. Appliqué the animals to the yellow blocks.

5. Use the embroidery floss in colors to match the print fabric to outline the animals with buttonhole stitches.

6. Chain-stitch the details. Satin-stitch mouths with red and outline the eyes with black.

7. Place each block, right side down, on a terry cloth towel and press.

8. Following the quilt plan, arrange the blocks. Sew the blocks together into horizontal rows, pressing the seams in opposite directions from row to row. Join the rows to complete the quilt top.

Finishing

Refer to "Quilt-Finishing Techniques" on page 77– 83.

1. Mark the quilting design onto the quilt top. The animal shapes were outlined. The green blocks were quilted with a grid of diagonal lines 2" apart. Oval and diamond shapes were used to fill the background space on some animal blocks.

2. Layer quilt top with batting and backing; baste.

3. Quilt and bind.

4. Sign and date your Animal Friends quilt.

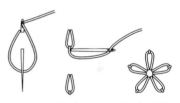

Detached Chain or Lazy Daisy Stitch

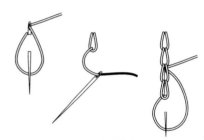

Chain Stitch

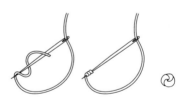

French Knot

Buttonhole Stitch

Satin Stitch

Embroidery Stitches

Reflection of Eagles

Paula A. Baimbridge is recognized for her appliqué quilts. Her designs are usually not traditional, however, and this quilt is no exception to her style. The design was replicated from a picture in a magazine. The original quilt was the property of the Henry Ford Museum in Dearborn, Michigan. It was destroyed in a fire in the museum in 1971. All that remains are photographs of the original, another good reason for making a replica.

The quilt features twelve eagles in two sizes with either nineteen or twenty tail feathers each, depending on the size. The eagles are made from drapery-weight cotton prints, with two eagles sewn in each of six color combinations. Notable fabric designs include paisley, a metallic gold print, and navy blue stars, accurately replicating the fabrics of an obviously patriotic quilt. The eagles are positioned around a wreath of flowers, with another flower in the center of the quilt. An elaborate swag-and-tassel border completes the dramatic design. Paula chose a low-loft polyester batting to give the appearance of an antique quilt. The dense background quilting of a grid of ¾" squares on point required six spools of quilting thread. This quilt was shown in several exhibits and has been awarded ribbons in various shows.

(Origin unknown) A picture of this unusual appliquéd quilt appeared in the November 1961 issue of Woman's Day magazine. (Photo courtesy of Henry Ford Museum, Dearborn, Michigan)

Reflection of Eagles by Paula Amelia Baimbridge, 1991, Midland, Texas, 93" x 93".

Finished Quilt Size: 93" x 93"
Setting: Medallion

Materials (44"-wide fabric)

8½ yds. off-white for background

2⅔ yds. (total) of 8 assorted decorator prints for small eagles (⅓ yd. each)

2 yds. (total) of 4 assorted decorator prints for large eagles (½ yd. each)

½ yd. (total) assorted solids for "combs" and beaks

2 yds. print for swags

2 yds. (total) scraps for tail feathers, swag fringe, and bird legs

¼ yd. green for leaves

¼ yd. for flowers

⅛ yd. for flower centers

8½ yds. for backing

1 yd. for binding

Embroidery floss in brown and green

Reflection of Eagles

Cutting

From the off-white background fabric, cut:

1 piece, 42½" x 96"
2 strips, each 28½" x 96"

Use the templates on the pullout patterns to cut the following appliqué pieces.

From the eagle prints, cut:

4 large eagle bodies
8 small eagle bodies

From the solids, cut:

4 large combs
8 small combs
4 large beaks
8 small beaks

From the swag fabric, cut:

24 swags
24 swag caps

From the green, cut:

4 center leaves
8 outer leaves

4 buds
24 leaves for beaks (total)

From the flower fabrics, cut:
5 flower petals
5 centers
4 buds

From the scraps for tail feathers, cut:
80 strips, each ¾" x 9", for large eagles
160 strips, each ¾" x 8", for small eagles
24 strips, each ¾" x 4", for feathers near feet
80 strips, each 1" x 8", for swag border
12 strips, each 1" x 1½", for eagle feet

Quilt Top Assembly

1. Sew one 28½" x 96" background strip to each side of the 42½" x 96" background piece. Press the seams open.

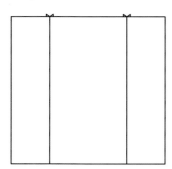

2. Fold the quilt top in half lengthwise, then crosswise. Press the folds lightly. Fold and lightly press diagonal lines to each of the corners. From the center, measure out 37½" on each side of the quilt top and mark lightly with pencil. From the center, measure 53" along each of the diagonal lines and mark.

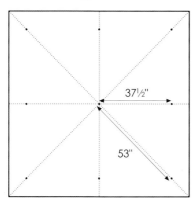

Mark all sides and corners.

3. Lightly draw lines to connect the marks on the quilt top, forming a square, 75" x 75", around which you will place the swag appliqués.

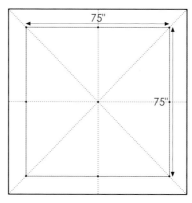

Mark all sides and corners.
Connect the marks.

4. Place the center flower and wreath pattern on a light table, then place the quilt top over the pattern. Line up the lengthwise and crosswise creases with the placement lines on the pattern and lightly trace the wreath outline and positions for flowers, leaves, and buds.

5. Using the "Basic Appliqué Methods," beginning on pages 74–75, prepare the appliqué pieces. Appliqué the center flower and wreath.

6. Position and pin or baste the large eagle body pieces in the corners of the quilt top as shown in the quilt plan, allowing room for tail feathers.

7. To prepare the tail feathers and feathers near the feet for appliqué, fold under ¼" on one end and press. Then fold both sides of the feather strips so that they meet in the center and press. The finished feathers are ⅜" wide.

❂❂❂❂❂❂❂❂❂❂❂❂❂ **NOTE** ❂❂❂❂❂❂❂❂❂❂❂❂❂

For a more rustic look, you may wish to make some of the tail feathers wider or narrower.

❂❂❂❂❂❂❂❂❂❂❂❂❂❂❂❂❂❂❂❂❂❂❂❂❂❂❂❂❂❂❂❂❂❂❂

8. Place tail feathers in a fan arrangement, two feathers near the feet, and a comb around the eagle's head, all with edges under the eagle body. Pin or baste all pieces in place and appliqué feathers, comb, and body in order. Place a beak on the eagle and appliqué. Appliqué two leaves at the point of the beak as shown on the appliqué pattern.

🮕🮕🮕🮕🮕🮕🮕🮕🮕🮕🮕🮕 **NOTE** 🮕🮕🮕🮕🮕🮕🮕🮕🮕🮕🮕🮕

Tail feathers can be overlapped slightly at the edge of the eagle body.

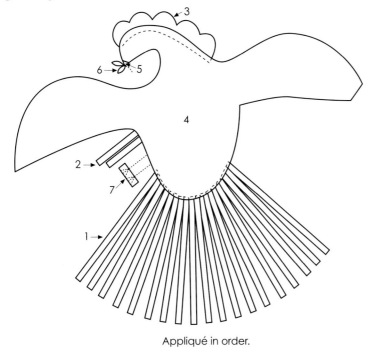

Appliqué in order.

🮕🮕🮕🮕🮕🮕🮕🮕🮕🮕🮕🮕🮕🮕🮕🮕🮕🮕🮕🮕🮕🮕🮕🮕🮕🮕🮕🮕🮕

9. For each eagle, trace the designs for the legs and the branch in the beak. Embroider the branches with chain stiches in green floss, and the eagles' legs in brown. At the ends of each eagle's embroidered legs, pin or baste a 1" x 1½" strip in place for the feet and appliqué. Embroider feet on the strips in brown floss.

10. Position small eagles between the large eagles and around the center wreath as shown in the quilt plan. Appliqué as for the large eagles.

11. Position 6 prepared swag appliqués on each side of the quilt top along the lines marked in step 3. Prepare the swag fringe strips as you did the tailfeather strips. Place 3 of the 1" x 8" strips between each pair of swag units. Pin or baste in place and appliqué swag fringe strips, then swag units. Finally, place swag caps between each pair of swag units, covering the fringe strips. Pin or baste and appliqué.

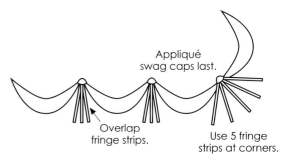

Appliqué swag caps last.

Overlap fringe strips.

Use 5 fringe strips at corners.

Finishing

Refer to "Basic Quilt-Finishing Techniques" on pages 77–83.

1. Mark the quilting design onto the quilt top. This replica was quilted with a grid of lines ¾" apart.
2. Layer the quilt top with batting and backing; baste.
3. Quilt and bind.
4. Sign and date your Reflection of Eagles quilt.

asic Quiltmaking Techniques

Replicating the old-fashioned patterns in this book will require the basic quiltmaking tools and skills described below.

Tools and Supplies

Today there are many wonderful tools and supplies that were not available to quiltmakers of the past. Use them for accurate results and to make your job easier.

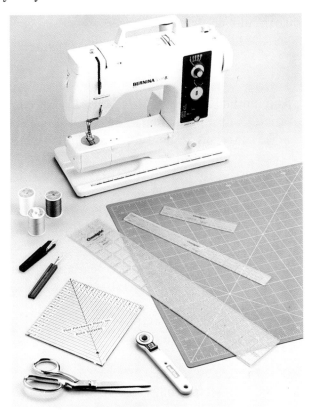

Rotary Cutter and Mat

Purchase the largest mat you can conveniently use and store. Treat yourself to a small mat for cutting scraps. Keep your rotary-cutter blade sharp with regular cleaning and a drop of oil. Loosen the screw and keep the pieces in order. Wipe away the lint with a soft cotton cloth, then smooth on a drop of oil. Reassemble the cutter in reverse order. Make a habit of closing the cutter when it is not being used. Keep a replacement blade handy.

Rulers

Choose rulers made of clear, hard acrylic specifically designed for use with rotary cutters. Some specialty rulers that are particularly useful include:

Bias Square®, 6" or 8" size—helpful for making half-square triangle units

ScrapMaster—a tool designed for cutting individual half-square triangles in a variety of sizes from scraps

Long ruler, 6" x 24"—helpful for cutting strips and borders

Acrylic square ruler, 12½" or larger

Sewing Machine

Clean and adjust your machine before starting a new project. Use a 70/10 or 80/20 needle with a universal point. I make it a habit to remove the throat plate and clean the "fuzzies" each time I put in a new bobbin. Cotton thread makes lint, and lint stops up the machine if it is not removed regularly. If cleaning at every bobbin change sounds often, do it after every two bobbins, and you will see how much lint accumulates. Wind several bobbins at a time so you can sew without interruption.

Quilting Thread

Cotton thread is best for use with vintage fabrics. Don't use vintage thread, as the strength is not trustworthy, and don't use polyester thread, which is too strong for vintage fabrics. It could damage them and is not authentic with older fabrics.

When quilting vintage tops or blocks newly set in tops, you may choose a color or colors, instead of just white or ecru. Many vintage quilts have multicolored thread showing in the stitches on the backings. The "Stars and Ninepatches" quilt in *Treasures from Yesteryear, Book One* was quilted with red, green, and cream.

Needles

For hand quilting, use Betweens #9 or #10; for hand appliqué, use a Sharp #12; for hand embroidery, use a #8 embroidery.

Pins

Keep plenty of fine straight pins on hand. The heavier pins make holes in vintage fabrics. I like having two containers so that one can be at the sewing machine and one at the ironing board.

You will need 200 to 300 size #1 nickel-plated safety pins for pin-basting the layers of a quilt together for quilting.

Iron and Ironing Board

Use a steam/dry iron and a spray water bottle. Keep an eye on the condition of the iron plate so no dye transfers from fabric to fabric. Use a layer of old sheeting to protect your ironing board cover when pressing vintage fabrics.

Marking Tools

A .5 mechanical pencil draws fine seam lines. A silver marking pencil is good for marking quilting lines. Tracing paper and graph paper in several scales help in planning quilts from vintage blocks. If you choose to make templates for some of the quilts, you will need template plastic.

Washing Products

Orvus® or Ensure are products that you can safely use on vintage fabrics.

Making Half-Square Triangle Units

Many traditional quilt patterns contain squares made from two contrasting half-square triangles. The short sides of the triangles are on the straight grain of fabric, and the long sides are on the bias. These are half-square triangle units.

Half-square triangle unit

Using a bias strip-piecing method and a special cutting guide called the Bias Square, you can easily sew and cut these units in many sizes. This tech-

nique, originally developed by Nancy J. Martin, is especially useful for small units, where pressing after stitching two small triangles together often distorts the shape. Another benefit of sewing in this manner is that there are no little seam-allowance "ears" to trim.

←— Seam allowance "ear"

It is easiest to cut bias strips from ⅓-yard or ½-yard pieces of fabric.

❈❈❈❈❈❈❈❈ **NOTE** ❈❈❈❈❈❈❈❈

You can cut bias strips from several fabrics at once. Layer the fabrics all with right sides facing up.

❈❈❈❈❈❈❈❈❈❈❈❈❈❈❈❈❈❈❈❈❈

The method shown here is Mary Hickey's adaptation as first published in her book *Angle Antics*. This method is ideal for scrap quilts where the background is all one fabric.

1. Using the 45° line on your Bias Square ruler, mark a bias line. Then use a long ruler to make a bias cut.

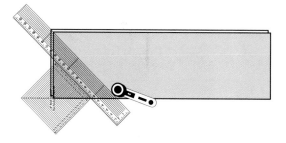

2. Cut bias strips the width required for your quilt pattern. In most cases, strips are cut the same width as the half-square triangle units. For example, cut bias strips 3" wide for 3"-wide half-square triangle units (cut size).

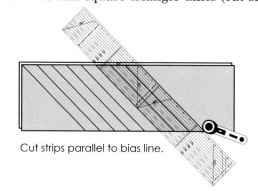

Cut strips parallel to bias line.

3. Sew the strips together with ¼"-wide seam allowances. Make bias panels of eight strips each. Alternate the fabrics in each bias panel, following the directions in the quilt pattern. Press the seam allowances toward the darker colors. On smaller half-square triangle units, press the seams open to distribute the fabric bulk. Keep the bottom edges as even as possible.

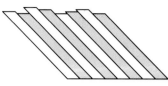

Sew bias panels.

4. Place the bias panel on your cutting board. Using a Bias Square, place the diagonal line on a seam line and position a long ruler as shown below to make a clean cut.

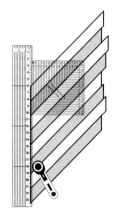

Use Bias Square
as a guide to
trim top.

5. Cut segments from the panel, cutting them the same width as you cut the bias strips to make the panel. If you cut 3"-wide bias strips, cut the segments 3" wide.

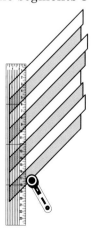 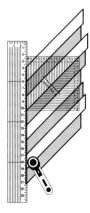

Make cuts same   Check angle
width as bias strips.   for each cut.

6. Sew the segments together end to end, taking care not to stretch the bias edges. This eliminates waste at the end of each strip.

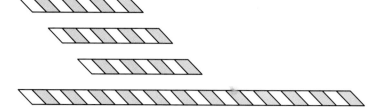

Join the segments to eliminate waste triangles.

7. Position the Bias Square with the diagonal line on the seam and one edge on the cut edge of the segment. Cut on one side.
8. Rotate the piece and align the Bias Square diagonal line on the seam. Cut again, completing the half-square triangle unit.

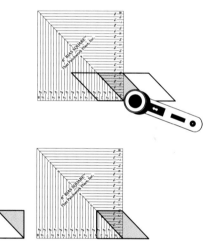

Rotate piece and cut second
side of half-square triangle unit.

⊠⊠⊠⊠⊠⊠⊠⊠   **NOTE**   ⊠⊠⊠⊠⊠⊠⊠⊠

For maximum efficiency, make all the cuts in one direction, then rotate the Bias Square and make all cuts in the other direction.

⊠⊠⊠⊠⊠⊠⊠⊠⊠⊠⊠⊠⊠⊠⊠⊠⊠⊠⊠⊠⊠⊠⊠⊠⊠

Basic Appliqué Method

Making Templates

Templates can be made from clear plastic or cardboard, but plastic templates are more durable and accurate. Since you can see through the plastic, it is easy to trace the templates accurately. Place template plastic over each pattern piece and trace with a fine-line permanent marker. Do not add seam allowances. Cut out the templates on the drawn lines. You only need one template for each different design in the quilt.

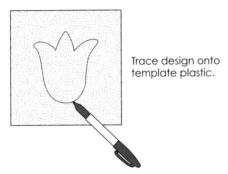

Trace design onto template plastic.

Marking and Cutting Fabric

Place the template right side up on the right side of the appliqué fabric. If several pieces are needed, leave at least ½" between tracings. Cut out each fabric piece, adding ¼"-wide seam allowances around each tracing. You will turn under this seam allowance to create the finished edge of the appliqué. On very small pieces, you may wish to add only ⅛" or a scant ¼" for easier handling.

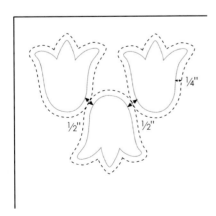

Leave at least ½" between templates.

The background fabric is usually a rectangle or square. It is better to cut the background an inch larger in each direction to start, then trim it to the correct size after sewing the appliqué in place, as appliqué blocks often "shrink" a little.

Mark the appliqué design onto the background fabric for proper placement. Place the fabric right side up over the pattern so that the design is centered. Use a pencil to lightly trace the design. If your background fabric is dark, use a light box, or try taping the pattern to a window or storm door on a sunny day.

Sewing Appliqué Pieces to the Background

Before sewing appliqué pieces to the background, turn under the seam allowance, rolling the traced line to the back. Baste around each piece. Try looking at the right side of the piece while you turn the edge under, basting right along the fold. This helps to keep the piece neat and accurate as you concentrate on the smooth shape of the piece. If you keep your stitches near the fold, you will be sure to catch the seam allowance.

Do not turn under edges that will be covered by other appliqué pieces. They should lie flat under the overlying appliqué piece.

Pin or baste the appliqué pieces to the background fabric. Small ½"- to ¾"-long sequin pins work well because they do not get in the way of the thread as you stitch.

⊠⊠⊠⊠⊠⊠⊠⊠   **N O T E**   ⊠⊠⊠⊠⊠⊠⊠⊠⊠

If you have trouble with threads tangling around pins as you sew, try placing the pins on the underside of your work.

⊠⊠⊠⊠⊠⊠⊠⊠⊠⊠⊠⊠⊠⊠⊠⊠⊠⊠⊠⊠⊠⊠⊠⊠⊠

Traditional Appliqué Stitch

The traditional appliqué stitch or blind stitch is appropriate for sewing all appliqué shapes, including sharp points and curves.

1. Tie a knot at the end of a single strand of thread approximately 18" long.
2. Hide the knot by slipping the needle into the seam allowance from the wrong side of the appliqué piece, bringing it out on the fold line.
3. Work from right to left if you are right-handed, or left to right if you are left-handed. Start the first stitch by moving the needle straight off the appliqué, inserting the needle into the background fabric. Let the needle travel under the background fabric, parallel to the edge of the appliqué, bringing it up about ⅛" away, along the pattern line.
4. As you bring the needle up, pierce the edge of the appliqué piece, catching only one or two threads.
5. Move the needle straight off the appliqué into the background fabric. Let your needle travel under the background, bringing it up about ⅛" away, again catching the edge of the appliqué.
6. Give the thread a slight tug and continue stitching.

 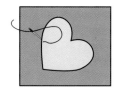

7. To end your stitching, pull the needle through to the wrong side. Behind the appliqué piece, take two small stitches, making knots by taking your needle through the loops. Check the right side to see if the thread will "shadow" through your background when finished. If it does, take one more small stitch through the back side to direct the tail of the thread under the appliqué fabric.

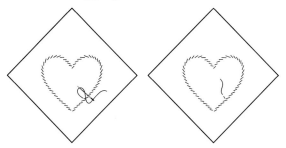

Assembling the Quilt Top

Straight Settings

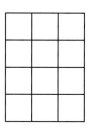

The easiest setting for quilt blocks is a straight one, with the blocks positioned side by side. Many of the quilts in this book require this simple setting.

1. Arrange the blocks in rows, following the quilt plan for pattern or color placement.
2. Sew the blocks together into rows, pressing seams one direction on odd-numbered rows and the opposite direction on even-numbered rows.

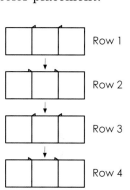

3. Stitch the rows together, matching the seams and easing any slight fullness.

"Animal Friends" on page 63 is sewn in a straight, side-by-side setting.

Diagonal Settings

Quilt blocks can also be joined in a diagonal side-by-side setting. This arrangement is also called setting blocks on point. A diagonal setting requires half blocks (side setting triangles) to fill in the edges, and quarter blocks (corner triangles) to finish the corners.

Side-by-Side Diagonal Setting

1. Arrange blocks, side setting triangles, and corner triangles in diagonal rows.

2. Join into rows. Press seams in one direction for odd-numbered rows and in the opposite direction for even-numbered rows.

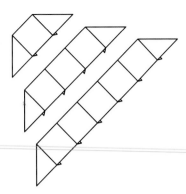

3. Sew the rows together, matching the seam intersections and easing as necessary.

4. Sew the corner triangles to the quilt top after joining the rows.

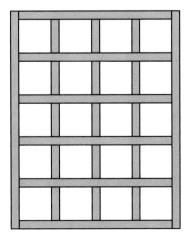

"Bars and Stars" on page 29 is sewn in a straight, diagonal setting.

Lattice Settings

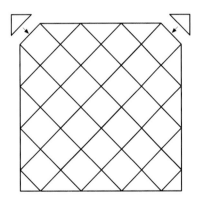

Side-by-Side Horizontal Setting
with Lattice

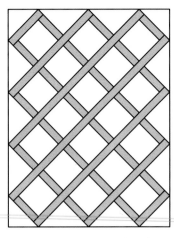

Side-by-Side Diagonal Setting
with Lattice

Adding lattice strips in either a straight or a diagonal setting enlarges the total project and separates the blocks. The "Railroad Crossing" quilt on page 43 was set with lattice between the blocks.

Straight Lattice Settings
1. Cut short and long lattice strips as directed for the quilt you are making.
2. Following the quilt plan, arrange the blocks into rows, with short lattice strips in between.

3. Sew the blocks and short lattice strips together and press the seams toward the blocks. (You may choose to press seams toward the lattice if lattice fabric is dark and would show through light-colored blocks.)

4. Before joining rows with long lattice strips, use a pencil to mark the following points on each edge: ¼"-wide seam allowance, finished lattice width, width of finished blocks, finished lattice width, and so forth, ending with a ¼"-wide seam allowance at the other end. These marks enable you to align the blocks accurately from row to row. Mark each long lattice strip.

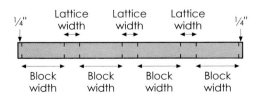

Mark long lattice strips.

5. Pin and sew the marked lattice strip to the row, matching the seams in the rows to the marks on the strip.

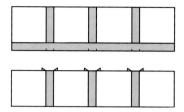

For additional information on a variety of straight and diagonal settings common in vintage quilts, see *Treasures from Yesteryear, Book One.*

Adding Borders

Borders with Straight-Cut Corners

1. After sewing the blocks together and pressing the quilt top, measure the width of the quilt across the middle and cut two border strips to match this measurement.

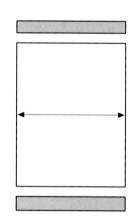

Measure and cut top
and bottom border strips.

2. Fold the quilt top in half lengthwise and mark the centers of the top and bottom edges of the quilt with a pin; fold and mark again into fourths and then eighths. Mark the centers of the border strips and divide them in the same fashion.

Match pins as you add the border.

3. Match the pins as you pin the top and bottom borders to the quilt top. Add more pins between the divisions as necessary to make sure borders are not stretched as they are stitched.

4. To add the side borders, measure the length of the quilt top across the center again, this time with the top and bottom borders included. Then, repeat the steps as for the top and bottom borders.

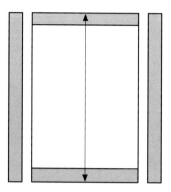

Measure and cut side border strips.

Quilt-Finishing Techniques

The following information will help you finish your quilts beautifully.

Planning Quilting Designs

Unfinished quilt tops really change character with the addition of quilting lines. Some "busy" scrap quilts look best with an old-fashioned shell design all over. Other, more formal quilt designs look best with feathers, wreaths, or hearts in the blocks, and cables, "punkin seeds," or grids in the borders and backgrounds.

Quilting designs are an important component of any quilt. The multitude of little stitches has two purposes. One is functional: connecting the top, batting, and backing with sufficient stitching to provide stability for the batting. Antique quilts with cotton batting were quilted heavily to maintain the evenness of the cotton batting and to keep it from shifting. Modern cotton batting can safely be quilted about 2" apart. More space between quilting lines can be left with current polyester battings.

A second purpose of the stitching is to provide a part of the overall design of the quilt. The quilting design should enhance the quilt pattern, attach the three layers of the quilt evenly, and be enjoyable to stitch.

The quilting design can be plain or fancy. Plain and simple outline quilting, also known as quilting "by the piece" (¼" away from the seam lines), is traditional for certain styles of quilts.

Other quilt styles require fancy quilting with feathers, wreaths, baskets, and other designs. Many quilts have a combination of these in the final design. The choice of quilting design for a quilt top made from vintage blocks ideally should be based on the styles of quilts made in the same period as the blocks. Consider the vintage fabrics when planning a quilting design. Simple outline quilting or in-the-ditch (in the seam line) quilting may be adequate for weaker vintage fabrics.

Close observation of quilting patterns on old quilts provides clues for quilting new replicas. Study the quilts in calendars and state quilt-documentation books for ideas. Find pictures of similar patterns. A magnifying lens is often helpful in revealing the quilting patterns.

Marking Quilting Designs

Quilting-in-the-Ditch   Outline Quilting

Outline quilting and in-the-ditch quilting follow the seam lines and do not require marking. Stencil patterns for blocks and borders and designs overlaid on patchwork can be marked with chalk or a silver marking pencil. Test the pencil on the fabrics that will be marked. Vintage fabrics may not release markers as well as new fabric. Use a gentle touch when marking, and if

the pencil does not erase as you quilt, try brushing the line with a scrap of polyester batting. Exact replication of some old quilts would leave the graphite pencil marks, but the best-looking quilts have no marks showing.

Choosing the Batting

The batting for a quilt with vintage fabrics can be 100% cotton or one of the new blends of cotton constructed in a polyester net. Either will be gentle on the vintage fabrics, yielding a quilt with the feel of an antique.

Flannel is another filler that was used in old quilts. It produces a very flat quilt but is difficult to hand quilt. Prewashing is essential for flannel as it shrinks considerably.

You may also choose a thin polyester batting for vintage quilt tops. The finished quilt will have the "flatness" of an old quilt even though quilting lines need not be spaced as close together as when using cotton batting. This is a real benefit for the more fragile vintage tops.

A regular-weight polyester batting provides a "fluffier" quilt with higher loft. This may be an appropriate choice for tops that have a good bit of fullness to "quilt out."

Layering the Quilt

1. Press the finished quilt top after adding the final border. Check the wrong side and "settle" any seam allowances that were pressed incorrectly.
2. Measure the width and length of the quilt. Cut and assemble the backing so that it extends 2" beyond the quilt top on all sides. Press seams open.
3. Check the batting package. Some cotton-blend battings require prewashing, and some polyester battings should be tumbled in a warm dryer to remove the fold lines.
4. Place the backing, wrong side up, on a large table or clean carpet.
5. Spread the batting over the backing and trim the batting to match the backing. Center the quilt top on the batting and backing. Starting at the center of the quilt, baste with large stitches or pin all three layers together with 1" safety pins. Working out

from the center, place lines of basting or pin about every 8".

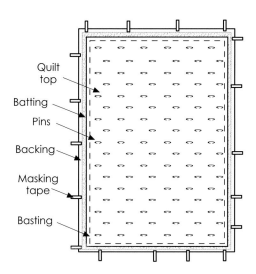

Quilt top
Batting
Pins
Backing
Masking tape
Basting

⊞⊞⊞⊞⊞⊞⊞⊞ **NOTE** ⊞⊞⊞⊞⊞⊞⊞⊞

Fold the backing over the batting and pin to "seal" the edges so the batting doesn't catch and pull away while you work.

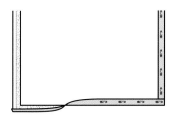

Fold edges to front and pin.

⊞⊞⊞⊞⊞⊞⊞⊞⊞⊞⊞⊞⊞⊞⊞⊞⊞⊞⊞⊞⊞⊞⊞⊞

Quilt according to the designs you have chosen, beginning in the center of the quilt. Continue to enlarge the quilted area from the center out. Work to make your stitches small and evenly spaced.

Quilting the Quilt

Traditional Hand Quilting

To quilt by hand, you will need short, sturdy needles (called Betweens), quilting thread, and a thimble to fit the middle finger of your sewing hand. Most quilters also use a frame or hoop to support their work. Quilting needles run from size 3 to 12; the higher the number, the smaller the needle. Use the smallest needle you can comfortably handle. The smaller the needle, the smaller your stitches will be.

1. Thread your needle with a single strand of quilting thread about 18" long; make a small knot and insert the needle in the top layer about 1" from the place where you want to start stitching. Pull the needle out at the point where quilting will begin and gently pull the thread until the knot pops through the fabric and into the batting.

2. Take small, evenly spaced stitches through all three quilt layers.

3. Rock the needle up and down through all layers until you have three or four stitches on the needle. Place your other hand underneath the quilt so you can feel the needle point with the tip of your finger when you take a stitch.

4. To end a line of quilting, make a small knot close to the last stitch, then backstitch, running the thread a needle's length through the batting. Gently pull the thread until the knot pops into the batting; clip the thread at the quilt's surface.

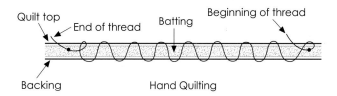

Quilt top   End of thread   Batting   Beginning of thread

Backing   Hand Quilting

For more information on hand quilting, refer to *Loving Stitches* by Jeana Kimball.

Machine Quilting

Machine quilting is suitable for all types of quilts, from crib to full-size bed quilts. With machine quilting, you can quickly complete quilts that might otherwise languish on the shelves.

Marking is only necessary if you need to follow a grid or a complex pattern. It is not necessary if you plan to quilt in-the-ditch, outline quilt a uniform distance from seam lines, or free-motion quilt in a random pattern.

1. For straight-line quilting, it is extremely helpful to have a walking foot to feed the quilt layers through the machine without shifting or puckering. Some machines have a built-

in walking foot; other machines require a separate attachment.

Walking foot

2. For free-motion quilting, you need a darning foot and the ability to drop the feed dogs on the machine. With free-motion quilting, you do not turn the fabric under the needle but instead guide the fabric in the direction of the design. Use free-motion quilting to outline quilt a pattern in the fabric or to create stippling and many other curved designs.

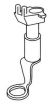
Darning foot

Free-motion quilting

To learn more about quilting by machine, refer to *Machine Quilting Made Easy!* by Maurine Noble (That Patchwork Place).

Finishing the Edges

The edge treatment can be an important part of the quilt design as well as contribute to the durability of the quilt. Make sure your fabric calculations include fabric for the type of binding or other edge finish you plan to use.

You may finish a straight edge without binding by bringing the quilt-top fabric to the back or bringing the backing to the front, turning in the raw edge and blindstitching it in place. Miter the corners as you go. This will work only if you have planned ahead, allowing enough excess backing or outer border to turn to the other side.

Self-Binding

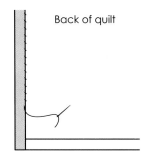
Bring front fabric to back.

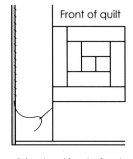
Bring backing to front.

If you plan to bring the backing forward, consider the impact of having the backing color at the outer edge of the finished quilt. Also, the edges of many old quilts with finishes of this type are worn through, with only one layer of fabric to take the wear. A double binding is a sturdier edge treatment. For my replicas of antique quilts, I use double-layer bindings rather than hemmed edges because the binding provides more durability, but I use colors consistent with the edge finishes of the old quilts. I use both straight-grain and bias bindings.

Binding strips may be cut on the straight of grain or on the bias. Straight-grain bindings are more common on quilts made before the mid-1920s, when designs with scalloped edges became popular. Bias binding is easier to apply for a smooth finish on curved edges.

You can sew decorative piping into a bias finish if you wish. Ruffles or folded squares called "prairie points" may also be added to decorate edges.

Quilts with irregular edges may require facing for a smooth finish. The Sunshine and Shadow version of Trip Around the World, the pieced "ice cream cone" border, and some Flower Garden edges (See *Treasures from Yesteryear, Book One.*) finish more easily with a facing.

Rotary-Cut Bias Binding

Before cutting binding strips, decide whether you want straight-cut or bias binding. Also decide whether you want to use single-layer binding or a double-layer binding. For a binding that finishes to ¼", cut single-layer strips 1⅛" wide. For a double-layer binding, cut strips 2" wide. If you prefer straight-grain binding, cut the binding strips across the fabric width or along the lengthwise grain, then join as shown.

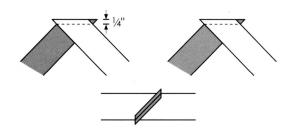

Rather than cutting individual strips that must be then joined into one continuous strip, use the following method, developed by Jackie Reis of Accu-Patterns.

Calculating Bias Binding

When you need more than a one-yard length of bias binding, use a calculator and the following method to determine the size of the square you need.

1. Find the distance, in inches, around the quilt: two lengths plus two widths.
2. Add 10" for mitering corners or curves and overlap.
3. Multiply this number by the width of the binding you plan to cut.
4. Find the square root. (Most calculators can perform this function.) Round the answer to the next highest whole number and add the width of the binding you plan to cut.

For example: The quilt measures 90" x 108".
- 90" + 108" = 198" (length plus width)
- 198" x 2 = 396" (distance around quilt)
- 396" + 10" (perimeter plus allowance) = 406"
- 406" x 2" (width of cut binding) = 812"
- Square root of 812 = 28.4956. Round up to 29" and add 2" to yield a 31" square of binding fabric.

Cutting Bias Binding

1. Cut a square of binding fabric the correct size, using the method above. Cut it in half diagonally.

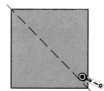

2. Place the pieces, right sides together, to form a "giant tooth." With edges even, stitch by machine, using a ⅜"-wide seam allowance. Press the seam open.

3. Place the fabric on the cutting board, with the wrong side of the fabric touching the board and the bias edges parallel to the length of the board.

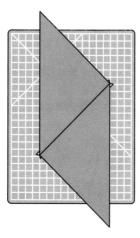

4. Fold the upper tip of the fabric down to the seam line; fold the lower tip up to the seam line so the straight-grain edges meet diagonally but do not overlap. This is the butting line.

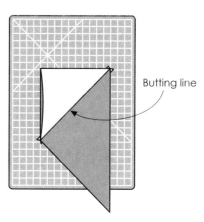

Butting line

5. Keep the bias edges even on the left side and as even as possible on the right. (Left-handed users, reverse these directions.) Fabric will be two thicknesses. Begin cutting the desired binding width from the left, using a rotary cutter, mat, and acrylic ruler. Stop the cutting 1" before you reach the seam line and start again 1" after it, so the cut will "jump" the line. Continue to cut across the width of the fabric with parallel cuts, jumping across the seam line on each cut. Cut through and discard the last incomplete row.

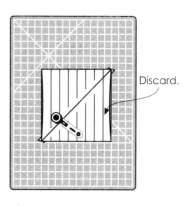

Discard.

6. Gently lift up the tip of the first row and use scissors to cut through to the end of the fabric. (See A+.) Gently lift up the tip of the last row and cut through to the end of the fabric. (See B.)

Gently slide and align the fabrics at the seam line so that A is even with A+ and B is even with B+.

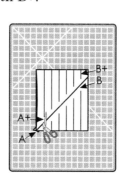

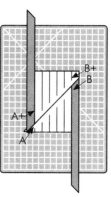

7. With right sides together, join butted edges together with a ⅜"-wide seam allowance, forming a tube.

8. Slide the fabric tube over the ironing board; press seam open. Using fabric scissors, cut across uncut portions of fabric, making a long, continuous strip.

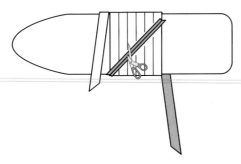

9. Unwind the bias strip from the ironing board.
10. For doubled binding, press the strip in half lengthwise with wrong sides together.

Attaching the Binding to the Quilt with Mitered Corners

1. Place the binding with the right side along the raw edge of the layered quilt. Sew the binding to the quilt, using a ¼"-wide seam allowance and stitching the binding to within ¼" of the edge of the quilt top. Backstitch to anchor the binding at that point.

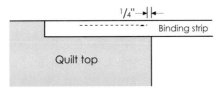

Backstitch ¼" from edge.

2. Fold the binding to the back of the quilt and finger-crease the binding at the fold.

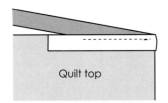

Crease binding.

3. Bring the creased fold to the top edge of the quilt corner, then turn down so the raw edge is even with the adjacent quilt edge. Begin stitching where the previous stitching

stopped. Back-stitch to anchor.

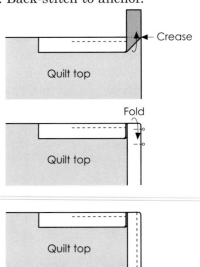

4. Continue to sew binding to the quilt edges, repeating steps 1–3 at each of the remaining corners.

5. Bring the binding edge to the back of the quilt. On the front, it will form a miter at each corner.

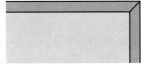

Front of quilt

6. On the back, the miter forms as you fold one side of the binding over the other and stitch to the backing as shown.

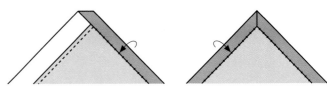

Back of quilt

Joining Binding Ends

To eliminate bulk where binding strips meet, join binding ends in a diagonal seam.

1. Stop stitching about 8" from where you began sewing the binding to the quilt. Binding tails should overlap several inches. Insert a straight pin into the quilt halfway between where stitching begins and ends.

Approximately 8"

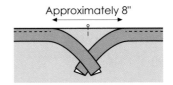

2. Pin the strips together (but not to the quilt) at the point where the pin is in the quilt. The binding should fit "comfortably" along the unsewn edge. Remove the pin from the quilt.

3. Measuring from the binding pin, cut the strips ½ the width of the binding. For example, if the binding was cut 2" wide, cut each strip 1" from the pin.

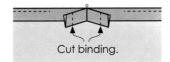

Cut binding.

4. Remove the binding pin, open the left strip (A) wrong side up, and open the right strip (B) right side up.

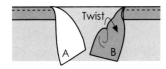

Twist

A B

5. Place end A at a right angle to, and on top of, end B. Stitch diagonally across the ends to form a triangle. Trim off the excess triangle, leaving a ¼"-wide seam allowance.

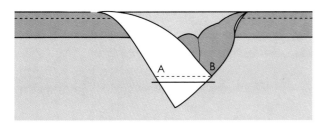

Sew ends together. Trim ¼" from seam line.

6. Finger-press the binding seam open. Refold on the fold line if using a doubled binding. The length of the unsewn binding should match the unsewn distance on the quilt. Stitch the binding to the quilt.

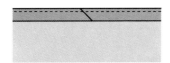

7. Fold the binding to the back of the quilt. Using thread to match the binding, hand stitch the binding to the quilt back.

Signing and Dating Your Quilt

Signing your quilt can be as simple as writing your name with a permanent fabric pen or as elaborate as your stitching skills will allow. The more information you provide about yourself and your quilt at the time you finish it, the better for your descendants and future quilt historians.

Include your name as quiltmaker (not just initials) and list your maiden name (often forgotten until the genealogy bug bites). Add the date the quilt was finished and the city and state where the quilt was made. Add information, such as the name of the pattern, the source of the design, or the name of the person for whom the quilt was made.

You can use embroidered or cross-stitched labels. Printed labels are also available for today's quiltmakers to record name, date, place, occasion, and other pertinent information. Permanent pens and detailed instructions allow you to personalize the labels, and there are new books to show you how to draw your own labels.

A name and date on an antique quilt may be hidden in the quilting and may require hours of searching. You may enjoy quilting your name within the quilting pattern of your quilt, and the fun may be in deciding how to disguise the letters in the quilting stitches.

All of the quiltmakers who remain anonymous in this book would have been named if they had signed their quilts.

Bibliography

Benberry, Cuesta Ray, and Carol Pinney Crabb. *A Patchwork of Pieces*. Paducah, Ky.: American Quilter's Society, 1993.

Beyer, Jinny. *The Art and Technique of Creating Medallion Quilts*. McLean, Va.: EPM Publications, Inc., 1982.

Brackman, Barbara. *An Encyclopedia of Pieced Quilt Patterns*. Lawrence, Kans.: Prairie Flower Publishing, 1984.

———. *Clues in the Calico*. McLean, Va.: EPM Publications, Inc., 1989.

Brandon, Ruth. *A Capitalist Romance: Singer and the Sewing Machine*. New York: J. B. Lippincott Company, 1977.

Finley, Ruth E. *Old Patchwork Quilts and the Women Who Made Them*. New York: Grosset and Dunlap, 1929.

Frost, Helen Young, and Pam Knight Stevenson. *Grand Endeavors: Vintage Arizona Quilts and Their Makers*. Flagstaff, Ariz.: Northland Publishing Company, 1992.

Fox, Sandi. *Small Endearments*. New York: Charles Scribner's Sons, 1985.

Garoutte, Sally, ed. *Uncoverings 1983*. Mill Valley, Calif.: American Quilt Study Group, 1983.

Goldman, Marilyn, and Marguerite Wiebusch. *Quilts of Indiana: Crossroads of Memories*. Bloomington, Ind.: Indiana University Press, 1991.

Gutcheon, Jeff. *A Quilter's Guide to Printed Fabric*. Tacoma, Wash.: Gutcheon Patchworks, Inc., 1990.

Hall, Carrie A., and Rose G. Kretsinger. *The Romance of the Patchwork Quilt in America*. New York: Bonanza Books, 1935.

Hickey, Mary. *Angle Antics*. Bothell, Wash.: That Patchwork Place, Inc., 1991.

Holstein, Jonathan. *The Pieced Quilt: An American Design Tradition*. Boston: Little, Brown and Company, 1973.

———. *Abstract Design in American Quilts: A Biography of an Exhibition*. Louisville, Ky.: The Kentucky Quilt Project, 1991.

Jenkins, Susan, and Linda Seward. *The American Quilt Story*. Emmaus, Pa.: Rodale Press, 1991.

Lasansky, Jeannette. *Bits and Pieces*. Lewisburg, Pa.: Oral Traditions Project, 1991.

———. *In the Heart of Pennsylvania*. Lewisburg, Pa.: Oral Traditions Project, 1985.

———. *Pieced by Mother*. Lewisburg, Pa.: Oral Traditions Project, 1987.

Levie, Place, and Sears. *Country Living's Country Quilts*. New York: Hearst Books, 1992.

The Lockport Quilt Pattern Book: Replicas of Famous Quilts, Old and New. Lockport, N.Y.: Lockport Batting Company, 1942.

Martin, Nancy J. *Threads of Time*. Bothell, Wash.: That Patchwork Place, Inc., 1990.

McMorris, Penny. *Crazy Quilts*. New York: E. P. Dutton, Inc., 1984.

Meller, Susan, and Joost Elffers. *Textile Designs*. New York: Harry N. Abrams, Inc., 1991.

Mills, Betty J. *Calico Chronicle: Texas Women and Their Fashions 1830–1910*. Lubbock, Tex.: Texas Tech Press, 1985.

Nelson, Cyril I. *Quilt Engagement Calendar*. New York: E.P. Dutton, 1990.

Newman, Sharon, ed. *Quilts of the Texas South Plains*. Lubbock, Tex.: Prairie Windmill Publishing, 1986.

Nylander, Jane C. *Fabrics for Historic Buildings*. Washington, D.C.: The Preservation Press, 1983.

Orlofsky, Patsy, and Myron Orlofsky. *Quilts in America*. New York: McGraw-Hill, 1974.

Peto, Florence. *American Quilts and Coverlets*. New York: Webster, Chanticleer Press, 1949.

———. *Historic Quilts*. New York: The American Historical Company, Inc., 1939.

Rehmel, Judy. *The Quilt I.D. Book*. New York: Prentice Hall Press, 1986.

Sandberg, Gosta. *Indigo Textiles, Technique and History*. Asheville, N. C.: Lark Books, 1989.

Schneider, Sally. *Scrap Happy: Quick-Pieced Scrap Quilts*. Bothell, Wash.: That Patchwork Place, Inc., 1990.

Schoeser, Mary. *Fabrics and Wallpapers: Twentieth-Century Design*. New York: E. P. Dutton, 1986.

Siegel, Beatrice. *The Sewing Machine*. New York: Walker and Company, 1984.

Webster, Marie D. *Quilts: Their Story and How to Make Them*. New edition. Santa Barbara, Calif.: Practical Patchwork, 1990.

Woodard, Thomas K., and Blanch Greenstein. *Twentieth Century Quilts 1900–1950*. New York: E. P. Dutton, 1988.

Notes

[1] Finley, *Old Patchwork Quilts and The Women Who Made Them*, p. 76.

[2] Hall and Kretsinger, *The Romance of the Patchwork Quilt in America*, pp. 238–39.

[3] *Ibid.*, p. 212.

[4] Nylander, *Fabrics for Historic Buildings*, p. 10.

[5] Peto, *American Quilts and Coverlets*, p. 46.

[6] Schneider, *Scrap Happy*, p. 7.

[7] Nelson, *The Quilt Engagement Calendar 1990*, plate 35.

[8] Brackman, *An Encyclopedia of Pieced Quilt Patterns*, p. 210.

[9] Schoesser, *Fabrics and Wallpapers*, p. 34.

[10] Gunn, "Dress Fabrics of the Late 19th Century," *Bits and Pieces*, p. 4.

[11] Mills, *Calico Chronicle*, p. 86.

[12] Webster, Marie D., *Quilts*, p. 102

[13] Pellman, Rachel and Kenneth, *How to Make an Amish Quilt*, p. 168.

[14] Sandberg, *Indigo Textiles, Technique and History*, p. 14.

[15] Bonta, "American Horticulturist," October 1985, p. 7.

[16] Meller and Elffers, *Textile Designs*, p. 174.

[17] Fox, *Small Endearments*, p. 1.

Meet the Author

Sharon L. Newman opened The Quilt Shop in Lubbock, Texas, in January 1979. In addition to teaching quiltmaking and presenting lectures about quilts and quilters, she appraises quilts and currently serves as administrator for the American Quilter's Society Appraisal Certification Program.

A charter member of both The American Quilter's Society and the American International Quilt Association, Sharon is also a member of the National Quilting Association and the Quilter's Guild of Dallas. She was a founding member of the South Plains Quilter's Guild and the Chaparral Quilter's Guild, both in Lubbock.

Sharon was curator for the 1986 Texas Sesquicentennial Quilt Exhibit in the Ranching Heritage Center, Texas Tech University, and editor of the exhibit catalog, "Quilts of the Texas South Plains." She is the author of *Handkerchief Quilts*, published in 1992.

Sharon was born and reared in Indiana. She is a graduate of the University of Texas, Austin, with a teaching degree in mathematics and English. She and her husband, Thomas, have lived in Lubbock since 1967. They have three daughters; Tracy Faulkner, Vicki Potts, and Carol Newman; one grandson, Clinton Thomas Faulkner, and two granddaughters, Taylor Alexandra Faulkner and Amanda Lea Potts.

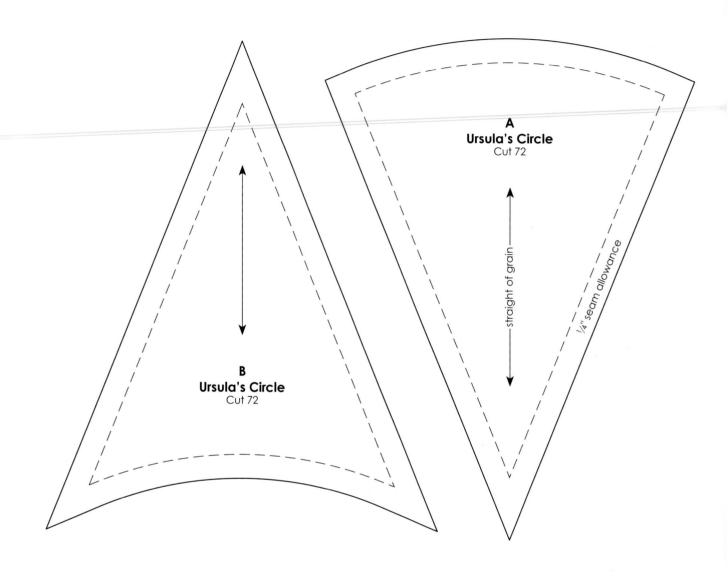

A
Ursula's Circle
Cut 72

B
Ursula's Circle
Cut 72

straight of grain

¼" seam allowance

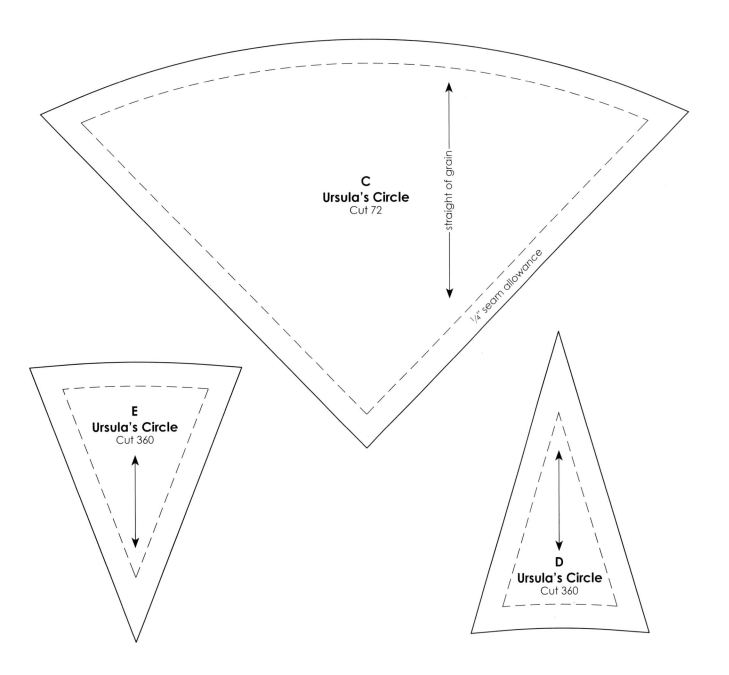

C
Ursula's Circle
Cut 72

straight of grain

¼" seam allowance

E
Ursula's Circle
Cut 360

D
Ursula's Circle
Cut 360

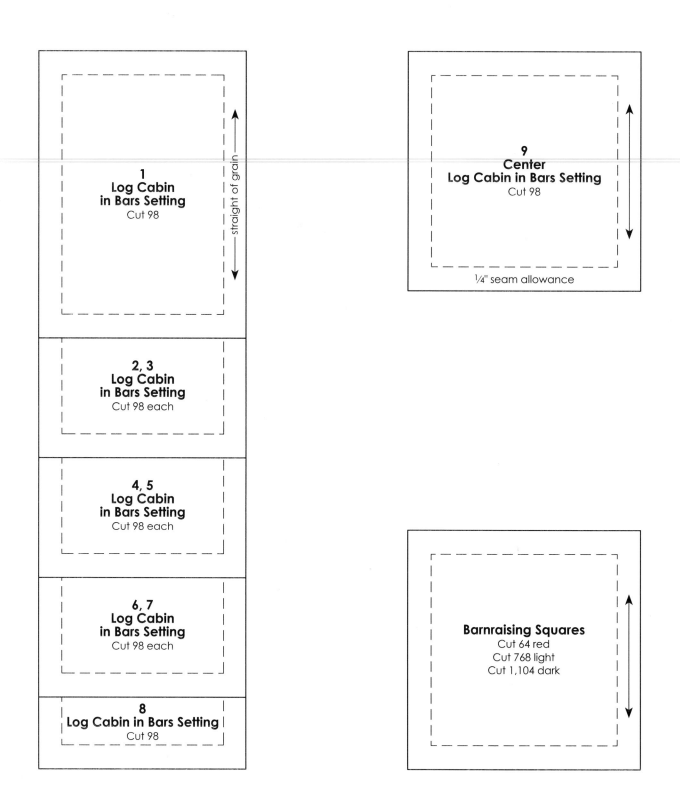

1
Log Cabin
in Bars Setting
Cut 98

straight of grain

2, 3
Log Cabin
in Bars Setting
Cut 98 each

4, 5
Log Cabin
in Bars Setting
Cut 98 each

6, 7
Log Cabin
in Bars Setting
Cut 98 each

8
Log Cabin in Bars Setting
Cut 98

9
Center
Log Cabin in Bars Setting
Cut 98

¼" seam allowance

Barnraising Squares
Cut 64 red
Cut 768 light
Cut 1,104 dark

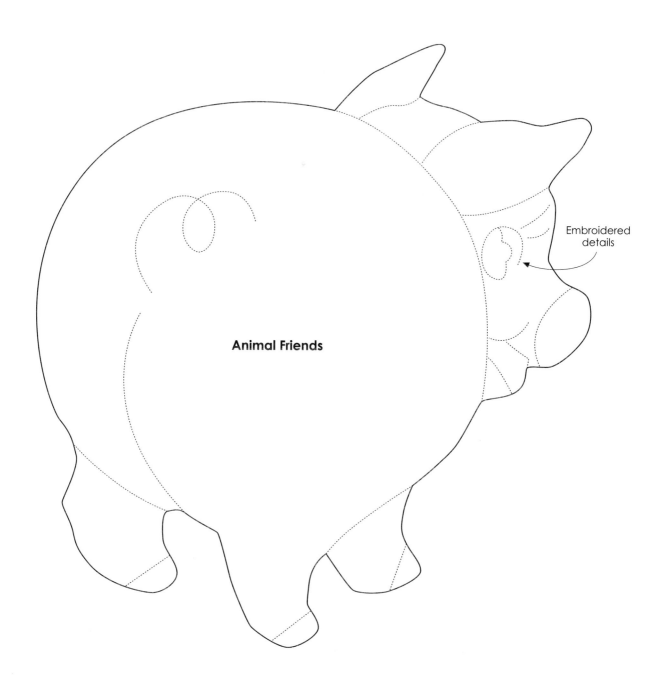

Animal Friends

Embroidered
details

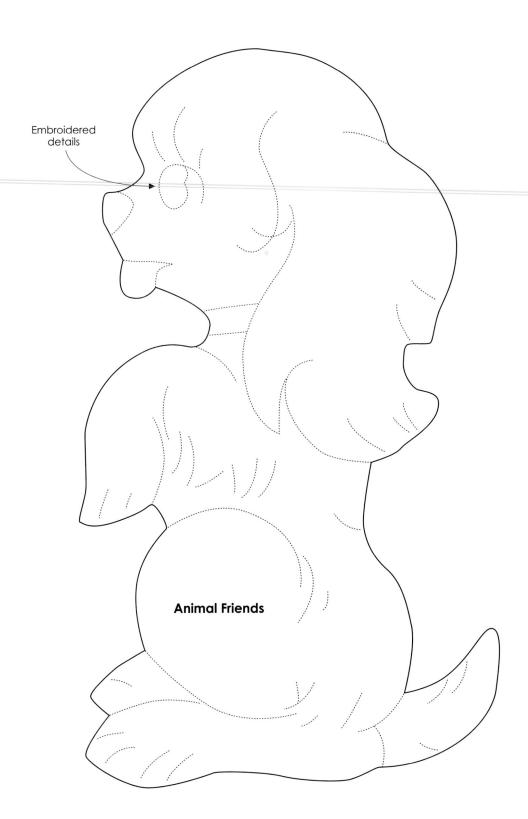

Embroidered
details

Animal Friends

Embroidered
details

Animal Friends

Embroidered
details

Animal Friends

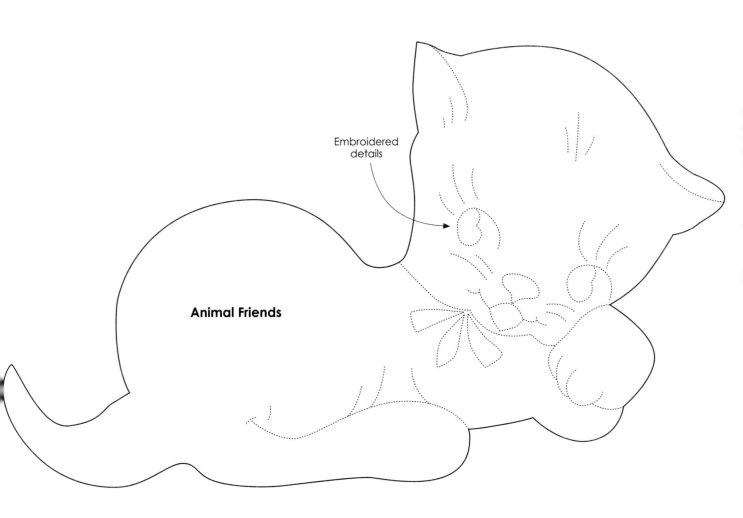

Embroidered
details

Animal Friends

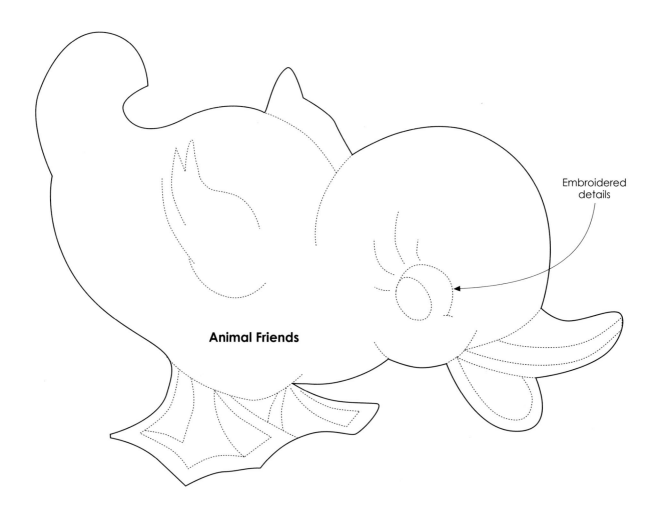

Embroidered
details

Animal Friends

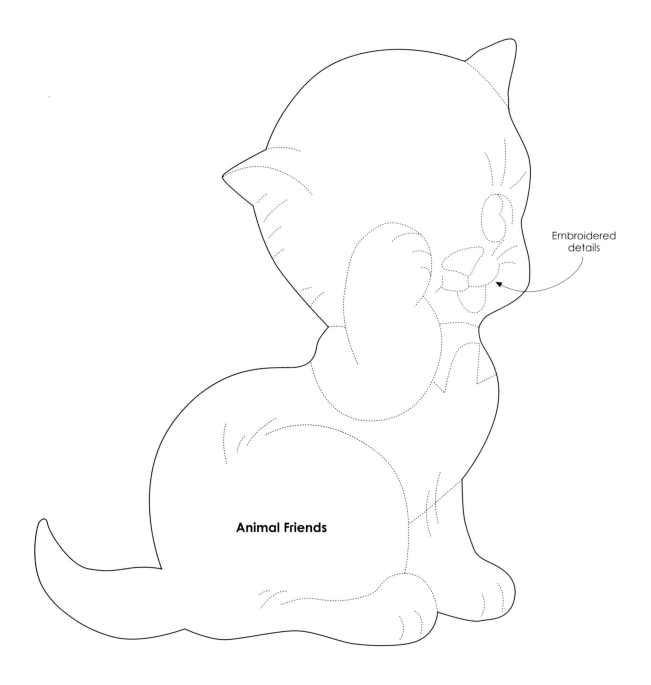

Embroidered
details

Animal Friends

That Patchwork Place Publications and Products

4", 6", 8", & metric Bias Square® • BiRangle™ • Ruby Beholder™ • Pineapple Rule • ScrapMaster • Rotary Rule™ • Rotary Mate™
Shortcuts to America's Best-Loved Quilts (video)

Many titles are available at your local quilt shop. For more information, send $2 for a color catalog to That Patchwork Place, Inc., PO Box 118, Bothell WA 98041-0118 USA.

☎ Call 1-800-426-3126 for the name and location of the quilt shop nearest you.